COPING WITH POSTNATAL DEPRESSION

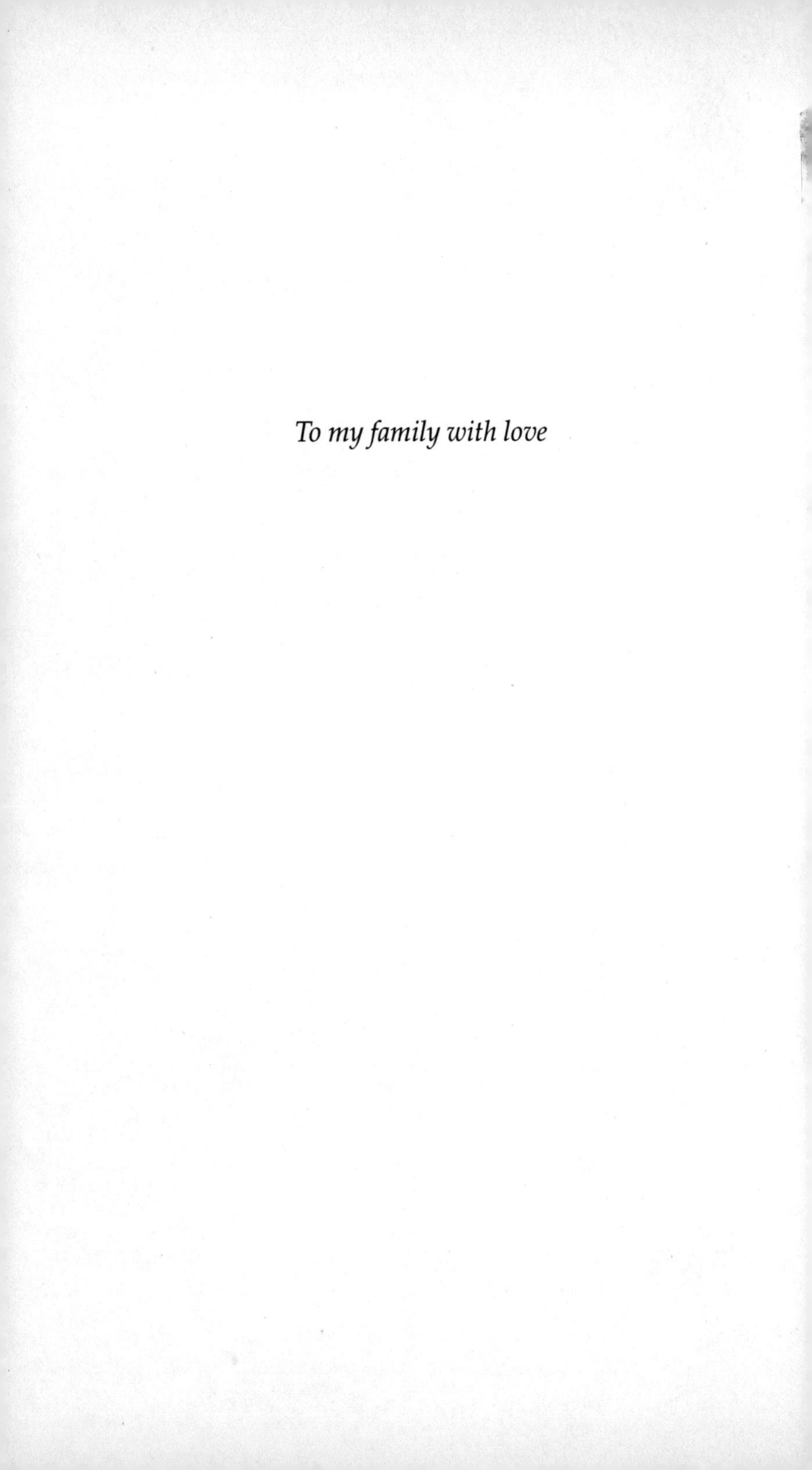

To my family with love

Mary Pigot

Coping with Postnatal Depression

LIGHT AT THE END OF THE TUNNEL

First published in 1996 by
the columba press
55A Spruce Avenue, Stillorgan Industrial Park,
Blackrock, Co Dublin

Cover by Bill Bolger
Origination by The Columba Press
Printed in Ireland by
Colour Books Ltd, Dublin

ISBN 1 85607 157 X

Contents

Preface

Sinead Cusack
Patron of the Association for Post-natal Illness

My first baby was born in September 1978. The omens were very good. I had a very happy pregnancy and can honestly say that I bloomed. I was very relaxed and enjoyed the whole experience. I had a home birth. It was an easy birth, and I'd go so far as to say it was an enjoyable birth.

My difficulties began with breast feeding. I felt that this was what all good mothers did, but I found it very painful in the early weeks and I believe that this was what triggered my depression. I was convinced that the baby was going to die because I felt that I wasn't feeding him properly. I began to feel so bad myself, that I was convinced that my milk could not be any good. However, I kept my feelings very secret. I felt that to tell people that I was uncomfortable breast-feeding would have meant that I was a failure. I became very depressed and introverted. I erected a wall around myself through which nobody could intrude. I felt bleak and desperate.

Like most of the sufferers in this book, nobody had warned me about the possibility of postnatal depression, so I did not recognise that this was what was wrong. Whenever I went to the baby clinic I was told that the baby was fine and everyone presumed that I was fine too. My depression affected me as guilt, panic, severe sweats and lack of sleep.

The illness went undiagnosed and therefore untreated. I kept it all a secret. My sisters and close friends perceived me as the original earth mother – and I was a good actress! My husband knew how bleak I was feeling, but he had never been a father before so he thought it was normal. Looking back I feel that if I had been given more help and information pre-natally , I would not have felt the guilt.

I have noticed a massive improvement in treatments and attitudes in recent years here in England. I gave a talk recently to doctors and psychiatrists and there is a much higher awareness of the dangers to mums and consequently the baby. Information and education are the most important needs and I am adamant that first time mothers must be made aware of the illness and the possibility that it will affect them. This would help greatly in releasing them from the feeling of isolation if they do go on to get PND. I sometimes think that there is a conspiracy amongst other women not to frighten off first time mums. I know that my own expectations of first-time motherhood were foolish.

This book is a vital step forward in the provision of education. The more that is written on the illness the more understanding there will be and the greater the relaxation for the mother. I hope that it will also be read by the professionals because a wider grasp of the whole question of the illness is important. It should be recommended reading for all first time mothers. One of the most important features of the book is that it tells you where to go to get help, and of course reading the stories of other sufferers lets you know that you are not isolated or alone.

The signs of PND are not pretty. The woman inside feels ugly but it is not a sign of an inner ugliness. I hope that this book will help to destigmatise the mental illness aspect of PND which manifests itself in ugly ways.

I would like to express my huge support for the Postnatal Distress Association of Ireland in all their work. My message to sufferers who are reading this book is simple: feel no guilt about the sensations you are suffering. It is not your fault.

Foreword

Dr Michael Turner
Master
Coombe Women's Hospital
Dublin

The arrival of a healthy newborn baby is usually romanticised with high expectations of joy and happiness. In reality, this is not always so. The majority of mothers experience feelings of unhappiness in the first few days after giving birth, and for a small number this unhappiness may be profound, leading to depression.

Postnatal depression is usually unexpected and often inexplicable. It invokes a strong sense of helplessness, not only in the mother herself but also in her partner, her immediate family and in those responsible for her care. As a gynaecologist, I have shared that sense of helplessness and, thus, I warmly welcome this book with its professional and deeply personal insights.

As well as the practical information provided, I believe that this book will give mothers a better understanding of their emotions after childbirth. It should also be read by anyone providing personal or professional support for women who are pregnant. In addition, I hope it will galvanise all of us responsible for the provision of women's healthcare into implementing further improvements in the services for mothers experiencing postnatal depression. In particular, the proper provision of mother and baby units nationally needs to be addressed. This book also highlights the need for additional research into the psychological impact of pregnancy on women and their families in an Irish context.

Finally, the publication of this book represents a personal triumph for many of the contributors. I admire their courage and I am proud to be associated with their endeavours.

What is Postnatal Depression?

Siobhán Barry MD, MRCPsych
Visiting Consultant Psychiatrist,
Coombe Women's Hospital

Flowers, visitors and greetings cards convey the excitement and joy that are popularly associated with childbirth, but the reality for many mothers is that their birthing experience leaves them feeling exhausted, tearful and disappointed. This is quite common but it is not something which is often spoken about or acknowledged. Consequently, when negative feelings arise in relation to childbirth, they are unexpected. There may be no opportunity to share such thoughts, leading to a sense of isolation, personal failure and shame.

With the influx of visitors to see mother and baby, couples can find themselves in something of a dilemma, wanting on the one hand to show off their new arrival with pride and delight, but also needing time to rest and the mental space to get used to their baby. Most maternity hospitals have a policy on the maximum number of visitors allowed per patient at any given time, but few actually enforce this. As a result, many mothers who deliver in hospital find that they are worn out from the hospital routine and that, in coping with the volume of visitors, they have had very little time to rest. Quite a few mothers who themselves go on to develop later postnatal mood problems link their difficulties with the fact that they could not relax in hospital because of a constant stream of well-wishers.

Expectations versus Reality

For first time parents, the reality of parenthood may fall somewhat short of their expectations. Despite having months of preparation for the arrival of their baby, many feel overwhelmed by a sense of responsibility which they had not fully expected. Many first time parents are also ill-prepared for the turmoil that comes in the wake of having a baby and may feel that this normal domestic upheaval is, in some way, due to their ineptitude. Few real-life mothers and their offspring can compare with the contented, serene images of motherhood which are portrayed in glossy magazines and brochures!

Lifestyle Changes

Changes in lifestyle and identity which accompany parenthood are greatest for women, particularly first-time mothers. Women who previously worked outside the home will now find themselves staying at home for the first time, even if this is merely for the duration of maternity leave. They may find that they have not yet established friendships in their neighbourhood, and may miss the companionship, status, freedom and financial independence that work brings. Conversely, women who plan to return to work after a period of maternity leave, may start to feel uneasy about this, and somewhat guilty that they might be perceived to be abandoning their child. This situation can be worse for those who, for economic reasons, have little choice in the matter of working outside their homes.

Relationship Changes

Psychological difficulties can emerge for couples following childbirth which have their origins at a much earlier point, either in their own lives, or in their relationship with their parents. Past emotional problems which have never been dealt with may surface. The arrival of a baby into a relationship can give rise to tensions between couples, as they adjust to the changes in their lives and attempt to attend to the considerable new physical demands made upon them. Differences of opinion may come to light between couples or involved grandparents or other relatives, regarding the care of the infant. Tactless, insensitive remarks by relatives can be taken up in a manner which can escalate into conflict across the generations.

Delays in attachment and bonding

After birth, most mothers expect to form an instant attachment to their child, and can feel confused and bewildered when this does not happen immediately. Up to 40% of mothers who have had a long and painful labour can be dismayed and distressed to find that they are numb emotionally when their child is finally presented to them. The memory of this can remain with them for a long time to come. Mothers who feel this way benefit from being gently encouraged to hold, talk to, cuddle and caress their baby as a way of maintaining physical contact, until their emotions unlock. It sometimes helps mothers to consider their relationship with their baby in the same way that one considers other intimate partnerships – sometimes it is love at first sight, but at other times, a lasting bond may take longer to develop.

On returning from hospital ...

The weeks and months following childbirth are not always characterised by mother's emotional well-being. During these months, couples need to adjust practically and emotionally to their increased responsibilities. The balance within a relationship alters with the arrival of a child, as do the couple's relationships with their own parents. Secure emotional attachment between the baby and key adults will form the basis for the child's future sense of self-worth and confidence, and her ability to develop both physically and intellectually.

Recognised Mood Changes

There are three main types of distinct postnatal mood changes which can affect mothers. These are: the maternity blues, postnatal depression and puerperal psychosis.

The closer the onset of any postnatal mood change to delivery, the greater the likelihood of hormonal factors in its causation. During pregnancy, the hormones oestrogen and progesterone are produced in quantities which are 200 times the amount produced in the non-pregnant state. Such increased quantities are necessary for the maintenance of the pregnancy. The immediate aftermath of childbirth is a time of enormous hormonal upheaval. There is a rapid shutdown in the amounts of oestrogen and progesterone produced, and an increase in the production of the hormone, prolactin, which will facilitate breastfeeding. These hormonal changes may also trigger a chain reaction of alterations in the neurotransmitter systems of the brain where one's mood state is regulated.

The Maternity Blues – Symptoms

Within the first week of childbirth, the spirits of two out of every three mothers plunge into tearful unhappiness and irritability. Other mothers will experience racing thoughts and a mild sense of elation which either occur on their own, or in association with the previously described tearfulness. Usually, this state of psychological disturbance begins within a few days of delivery, and lasts for a day or so. This condition arises irrespective of whether mothers deliver their babies at home or in hospital, but it is found to be more common in those who also suffer from premenstrual tension.

Maternity Blues – Treatment

Generally, this state resolves without specific treatment. It can be helpful to inform women before the birth that the maternity blues could arise so that they are not unduly distressed when it occurs. Low-key supportive care and understanding are beneficial to mothers while this is settling down. In about one fifth of cases the maternity blues may persist, and develop into a more severe psychiatric disorder.

Maternity Blues – Causes

While the origin of the maternity blues is by no means certain, there is research evidence that a particular amino acid, tryptophan, is reduced in those who develop the maternity blues, and this lack has also been described in those who suffer from non-pregnancy related clinical depression. It is likely that there is some association between the sudden decline in the production of naturally occurring progesterone in the days after delivery and diminished tryptophan levels.

Puerperal Psychosis — Symptoms

The most serious form of mood disorder, which fortunately is also the rarest, is puerperal psychosis, which affects one to two per thousand mothers.

This is a major mental condition of relatively sudden onset which begins with mild confusion and insomnia within the first week to month after delivery, and usually after a period of relative well-being and normality. The initial symptoms can very quickly and catastrophically progress. With the increasingly shorter periods of time that women now spend in maternity hospitals, many cases arise at home, to the bewilderment of patients, their partners and their families.

Mothers who undergo a puerperal psychosis are confused and irrational in their thinking patterns. They are often extremely fearful and may believe that the world around them has become strange and threatening. In this frame of mind, their senses may become disturbed and they may have unwarranted concerns about their own and their baby's health and safety. A woman may believe that both she and her baby are the victims of some dangerous plan. Threatening voices may echo in her head confirming this terrifying situation, and can lead to suicidal and homicidal gestures and attempts. Generally mothers in this state become easily distracted, disorganised in behaviour and experience a profound difficulty in sleeping due to the persistence of terrifying racing thoughts. It is not possible to reassure someone in this state that they have nothing to fear, as any comforting reassurance is short lived in duration.

Puerperal Psychosis – Treatment

The close monitoring, security and specialised care which this condition requires cannot, in general, be provided at home or in a maternity hospital, and psychiatric hospitalisation is necessary for treatment. Such mothers may need to stay for weeks or months. The condition usually responds well to drug treatment and/or electroconvulsive treatment, and mothers can make a full recovery. A full state of well-being may take some time, and often only returns after discharge home.

Ideally, mothers suffering from puerperal psychosis should be admitted to a specialised mother-and-baby unit where psychiatric nursing skills are available to the mother, and initially closely supervised mother and baby contact is allowed so that maternal attachment and bonding are promoted. The provision of such treatment is virtually non-existent in Ireland, and the continuance of this type of care is under increasing threat in Britain, with the closure and amalgamation of regional mother-and-baby units.

Puerperal Psychosis – Causes

Puerperal psychosis tends to occur more commonly, but not exclusively, in those who have a previous personal or family history of manic depressive illness, schizophrenia or puerperal psychosis. There is certain research evidence to support the belief that plummeting oestrogen levels in the postnatal period bring about a sequence of compensatory alterations in brain chemistry, which eventually leads to psychosis. Difficult social circumstances or problems in delivery have not been found to be specifically associated with this disorder, and it occurs in all cultural settings.

Puerperal Psychosis – Recurrence

Puerperal psychosis has a recurrence rate of 50% following subsequent deliveries, although this is diminished somewhat by increasing the time span between one pregnancy and the next. Mothers who develop puerperal psychosis have a 20% chance of relapsing with a similar, although usually less severe state of mood disturbance, at another non-pregnancy related time in their lives.

Puerperal Psychosis – Prevention

It is not yet possible to predict, in advance of delivery, which women will suffer from puerperal psychosis. Consequently, it is only those who are known to be at risk of puerperal psychosis who can benefit from preventive strategies. As previously mentioned, those at risk of suffering from puerperal psychosis have a personal or family history of manic depressive illness, schizophrenia or previous puerperal psychosis. Women with such a history need to disclose this to their obstetrician so that early warning signs of becoming psychotic are picked up, and treated early.

It is also possible to start a course of medication, for example lithium or a low dose of a major tranquillising drug, immediately after delivery, in an effort to reduce the likelihood of a relapse of puerperal psychosis. Women who opt for this will not be able to breast-feed, as such preparations are secreted in breast milk. There is evidence that such preventive action can reduce the likelihood of recurrence, or can diminish the intensity of an episode, were it to happen again. As 80% of cases of puerperal psychosis will have arisen within 6 weeks of delivery, preventive medication is generally tailed off after this time, particularly if there has been no evidence that the condition has re-emerged in a modified form.

Postnatal depression

The most common medical condition linked to childbirth is postnatal depression. Postnatal depression occurs more frequently but is less dramatic and less potentially serious than puerperal psychosis. It appears to be a condition which is only described in advanced Western type cultures (see below), and in this, it is also differentiated from the maternity blues and puerperal psychosis.

What is postnatal depression?

Postnatal depression is the term used which loosely covers a range of emotional states, from that of an adjustment reaction to parenthood to the development of a more profound state of anxiety and misery arising after a woman has a baby. For the majority of mothers, this state of unease clears up of its own accord within a number of weeks and formal treatment is not required. For a smaller number of women, the condition persists and gets worse.

Postnatal depression usually, although not always, arises within weeks or months of delivery, at a time when the mother has left hospital to resume her life. With postnatal depression, women feel unrelentingly tired, cannot relax, sleep poorly, are unable to enjoy life and become low spirited. Their inability to sleep occurs irrespective of how the baby sleeps. Food ceases to be enjoyable and many mothers lose a marked amount of weight. Often, women become irritable, particularly with their partner, and their interest in sex diminishes with a consequent strain on their relationship. They may become worried about their child's well-being, and often their confidence is so low that they constantly seek reassurance from their family doctor or public health nurse by asking to have the baby's development checked. Generally, their baby is thriving physically, but nobody asks the mother how she is feeling and how well she feels she is coping.

Who gets postnatal depression?

Postnatal depression affects more than one in ten mothers in Western Europe, and in one third of cases will last for more than 12 months, particularly if it is unrecognised and untreated. In Dublin, a study carried out at the Rotunda Hospital by Dr Mary Martin in the 1970s found that 14% of mothers were significantly depressed six weeks after their baby was born. Two decades later, in 1994, a study carried out by Dr Abbie Lane, at the Coombe Women's Hospital, found postnatal depression in 12% of mothers.

The possibility that postnatal depression might arise is not typically raised with prospective parents in the antenatal setting. It is essential that they are educated and informed of this state, of the frequency with which it occurs and that they know how they might look for help should it happen. It is important that they are also aware that it resolves with support and that sometimes short-term drug treatment is required. Two percent of those who develop postnatal depression will have a condition of a severity that hospital admission will be required.

Women who become depressed or very anxious during pregnancy have a high likelihood of experiencing postnatal depression after their baby is born. These women need closer support because of this vulnerability. Research studies on postnatal depression show that those who go on to become depressed postnatally tend to experience more difficulties with their pregnancy, have marital or relationship difficulties and are often at a social disadvantage with poor social supports. Being a single parent is a risk factor, particularly if this mother is unsupported by friends and family. Those whose pregnancies were unplanned and, almost paradoxically, mothers who have had difficulties conceiving also tend to be at a higher risk of developing postnatal depression.

Women who are bottle-feeding and taking the oral contraceptive pill are more likely to be depressed, followed by those who are fully breast-feeding. Those who combine both breast and bottle feeding tend to have the lowest rates of postnatal depression. Women who do not have an intimate, confiding relationship with their partner tend to be more vulnerable to depression in general, and to postnatal depression in particular. Women who have three or more children under the age of fourteen are also more prone.

Factors associated with postnatal depression

Women, irrespective of whether they have children or not, are more likely to suffer from depression. Does childbirth increase a woman's vulnerability to depression? Is postnatal depression due to hormonal factors, due to faulty thinking patterns, or related to the way women's lives are organised and the amount of practical and emotional support they receive?

The one consistent and significant link found in the literature on postnatal depression is that women who have a poor relationship with their partner tend to suffer. This is not to suggest that interpersonal difficulties between couples cause the problem, but they may have a part to play in postnatal depression manifesting itself. The nature of the deficiencies in the relationship have not been universally described but they can vary from father's being of little practical help in caring for the baby, to shortcomings in terms of communication, appreciation and demonstration of affection between the couple.

While hormonal factors have not been implicated in the development of postnatal depression, there is some evidence that a small number of cases may be triggered off by a decline in the efficacy of the thyroid gland which can arise after giving birth. This could be the explanation for postpartum depressive illness in a subgroup of women who have no adverse social or psychological factors. Apart from this link between thyroid dysfunction and mood changes, there is little evidence that other hormonal factors play a part in the development of postnatal depression.

Who doesn't get postnatal depression?

In societies where there is a recognised rite of passage to motherhood, e.g. in many primitive non-industrialised societies, or those which have developed technologically but have also retained many traditional customs, e.g. Japan, postnatal depression is virtually unknown. In these societies, there is a recognised ritual of enforced seclusion and rest for the mother after childbirth, while the extended family all expect to participate in childcare. This gives the mother time to recover from the physical effects of childbirth, and also time to adjust emotionally. After a fixed period of time, generally a month to six weeks, the mother returns to her own domestic life and takes up her maternal duties. This would suggest that some means of mandatory caring and support for the mother, to ensure that she gets the necessary help and rest after she has had a baby, guards against postnatal depression arising. By taking this form of action, there is an implicit understanding that mothers need practical and emotional help after childbirth, and mothers accept this help without feeling undermined.

Impact of postnatal depression on the family

Despite all the misery it can cause, postnatal depression is not considered to be a major mental illness for mothers. The impact of a depressed mother on the emotional, social and intellectual development of her child has not been widely studied and the long-term implications of this condition may be subtle and underestimated. The physical separation of mother and baby through maternal illness can hamper the bonding and attachment process. However, when no actual separation occurs, the quality of a mother's interactions with her child is also important, and a mother who is depressed and preoccupied with internal gloomy matters may not be able to provide her child with adequate emotional stimulation.

There is some evidence that the children of women with postpartum depression have behavioural problems later on in life. The ability of a mother to respond appropriately to her child has been found to be important to the child's intellectual and social development. Maternal mental illness may adversely affect her infant through neglect if the mother is depressed, apathetic and lacking in emotional warmth, or even physical harm if the mother is impulsive and chaotic.

More recently, evidence is also emerging of the likelihood of fathers also being affected, particularly if their partner suffered from postnatal depression.

Postnatal depression – Treatment

Mothers in the months prior to, and following, childbirth are in regular contact with various health professionals and it is crucial that they are alert to the emotional difficulties which can arise at this time so that the necessary help is made available.

Only about a quarter of those with postnatal depression whose suffering is of a severity that they seek formal psychiatric help, are prescribed medication. The symptom pattern and the domestic circumstances of the mother need to be taken into consideration when prescribing anti-depressants. For those with a marked inability to sleep, a sedating anti-depressant can be helpful, but clear instructions must be given that the partner or another responsible person will need to be available to attend to night feeds etc, under these circumstances. In other situations, newer, non-sedating anti-depressants which will not affect the mother's alertness might be indicated. Those who need medication may have to take this treatment for a six to nine month period. That anti-depressants may take at least two weeks before they begin to work, and any possible side effects of the medication prescribed, also need to be carefully explained and understood. Sometimes, when such medication is necessary, women may need to stop breast feeding, as the medication may be passed to the infant in breast milk.

To focus treatment totally on medication and solely on the postnatally depressed mother is of certain, though slight worth. It is of paramount importance that the partner is also engaged in joint treatment endeavours. Involving fathers in practical helping strategies or increasing their awareness of the importance of relating more effectively and more supportively to their depressed partner is of immense overall benefit. Men generally value the opportunity to gain a better understanding of what is going on and are also relieved that they can be of help in resolving matters. Frequently, the problem appears to be that men are quite willing but inexperienced in matters of babycare and household chores. Depressed mothers often have a difficulty in asking for practical help, and feel a failure if they accept it. Another common problem appears to relate to the impatience women have with the clumsiness and slowness of their partner's domestic skills. Many women feel that they would be better to do the chores themselves. Helping couples focus on their complementary styles, on being mutually supportive and on approaching the challenge of parenthood as a team is the way forward to their mutual betterment as parents, and as a couple.

Women who become depressed postnatally are helped by knowing the extent to which this condition arises, and also by meeting others who have had similar experiences, have survived them and have the confidence to share this. Self-help and support groups, such as the Postnatal Distress Association of Ireland (PNDAI) are of immeasurable benefit in this regard and their value is recognised at government level with the provision of limited funds for administrative backup. The availability of an emergency telephone line, social events, lectures and a quarterly newsletter are a welcome development of the 1980s.

In Ireland, a scheme of Community Mothers was also developed in recent years, comprising experienced mothers who are available as supports to women during the initial phases of negotiating their way through childrearing. Public health nurses have the necessary information on the local corps.

Finally, women will continue to become depressed after childbirth although if we raise awareness about this, much of the misery and isolation of postnatal mood problems will be avoided.

Experiences of Postnatal Depression

Mary

In July 1990 all my dreams came true. I was pregnant. I went to two GPs to be absolutely sure I wasn't dreaming. I really was on a high.

I remember being very nervous on my first visit to the hospital, but everything went well and once that was done I could tell people the news.

So now I ask myself, as I've asked so many times: Where did it all go wrong? I guess every woman who has had PND asks herself that same question over and over again. Could I have avoided it? Was it my fault? Why me? Having given the matter a lot of thought over the years since my PND, I guess the seeds were being sewn around half way through my pregnancy.

I'm a teacher and found that year the most stressful of my career. I let it all get on top of me. My husband, David, would often come home to find me lying on the couch in floods of tears over an incident that had happened in school that day. Nothing he could do or say seemed to relax me and I became more and more unhappy at work. My positive attitude to my pregnancy slowly began to change. I thought my morning sickness had come back. Now I know enough to say that I was getting sick with anxiety. Suddenly I no longer wanted to be seen in my pregnant state. I remember being at a wedding when I was six months pregnant and someone saying to me that I was huge. This didn't help my already eroded self-confidence and I went out even less after that.

At about seven months I began to feel very uncomfortable. I know most pregnant women feel like this but I was at my wit's end. No matter how I sat or stood I was uneasy in myself and very self-conscious.

We spent the first weekend of my maternity leave in Cork and on the way home we stopped at a pub in Tipperary for some lunch. I went to the toilet and realised to my horror that my waters had broken. I nearly collapsed with shock as my baby wasn't due for another three weeks. Never in my wildest dreams did I expect this. I hadn't a clue what to do. We asked for directions to the nearest maternity hospital and set off. After an internal examination and a call to the Coombe Women's Hospital I was let go. I was so shocked at this stage my lips were numb.

After what seemed like an eternity we arrived at the Coombe. My doctor explained that if I didn't go into labour naturally that night I would have to be induced the following day. The day came and went and I hardly dilated a centimetre. I was on the epidural and kept having to get topped up. I'm sure the anaesthetist on call that night would have happily strangled me. My husband was sent home to bed and I spent another night without sleep.

When the nurse examined me at about 3.30am I was fully dilated and ready to give birth. I remember no pain while giving birth. I do remember the elation I felt when we were told it was a boy. To say I was on a high was somewhat of an understatement. I had moved onto another planet. I felt somewhat removed from the situation, like someone viewing the happy family through a window. When the much publicised cup of tea came I couldn't face it. Instead I asked for a bowl, and proceeded to get sick.

My stay in the hospital is in one way vivid in my mind, and in another a complete haze. I remember waking and realising that I'd finally done it, I'd given birth. However, things were happening to me that I wasn't really prepared for. I was shocked at the amount of blood I was losing but far worse than that was the total indignity of being unable to go to the toilet. I had to beg the nurse for a catheter.

At one stage I was visited by a paediatrician who asked where my husband was and I said he was at work. The paediatrician then proceeded to tell me in medical jargon that David was low in calcium and jaundiced being premature, and that he would have to go up to the Baby Unit for treatment. It was the manner in which this information was relayed to me that tipped me over the edge. As far as I was concerned my baby was going to die. I saw a picture of a little white coffin going into the dark earth. I told no-one of my fears. Communication of the problem in layman's terms and the presence of a nurse to answer any questions I may have had, could have saved me much agony.

I was swamped by visitors from morning to night. One night I 'held court' to fourteen people in my room. Nobody would have had a clue that behind the smile and bravado was a new mother in total despair. I was given a lovely outfit for David by one kind visitor for when he would reach 18 months. I just said to myself 'Why? Sure he'll be dead long before then'.

More sleepless nights followed. I wandered the corridor and even visited the nursery at 4am, desperate to sleep but unable to relax. Eventually I was persuaded to take a sleeping tablet. I was so frightened that I asked my Mum to stay with me until I slept. I asked her to look after my two Davids if I died that night. The books talk of the three day blues. Boy did I get them. The flood gates opened and I cried buckets of tears. I wouldn't let David go back to work and clung to him like a child. The sister in charge came to see me and suggested I stay an extra night. I was delighted. If the truth be known I was terrified at the thought of going home with my new baby.

The first few days at home are hazy and jumbled in my mind. I do remember being swamped with visitors, not sleeping and being in a high state of anxiety. I was unable to make even the simplest of decisions. If the baby even dribbled a tiny bit of milk out of his mouth, I panicked. I stopped eating, and coping with the house was just beyond me.

Then it all came to a head. I had literally crawled up the stairs to bed, comatose with exhaustion, when the doorbell rang. I came back down to see a man hand in a beautiful bunch of flowers. I came to the bottom of the stairs and fell into a heap on the floor in front of my husband. I was in a desperate state and we didn't know what to do. We rang the hospital and they said either to come back in or ring our GP. It seemed easier to call our GP so we did that. He came and put me to bed with a shot to help me sleep. I could hear him downstairs telling David that I had PND. That is the first time I ever heard of the illness. He wrote a prescription for anti-depressants and left.

The following day my public health nurse came, no doubt alerted by my GP. She didn't seem to be able to offer me any help or information. She seemed as mystified as the rest of us. I guess everyone thought I would recover quickly.

David was left to look after the baby at night while I slept in the spare room, full of tablets. One morning he came in holding the baby in his arms. The baby was crying and he couldn't stop him. My heart nearly broke. I felt so useless. Now the two of us were exhausted and he had to go to work every day with all this worry on his mind. What was supposed to be such a happy time was turning into a hideous nightmare.

The minute David left for work each morning I got a panic attack. I'd phone him to come home, or phone Mum who would spend the day with me until David came home. This became a regular occurrence and my mother spent most of that summer with me. My sister came and did the night feeds for a few weeks which meant David could get some sleep, but I wasn't getting any better.

At my six week check up my gynaecologist, who was unaware of my illness, was shocked at what he saw. He spoke to David and by the end of that meeting I had decided to move back to my parents' home.

I stopped taking the anti-depressants but there was no improvement. My depression worsened. On another visit to my gynaecologist he suggested I see a psychiatrist. Our first few sessions seemed like a waste of time to me. I cried a lot and didn't feel any better. Now I know how therapeutic all that crying was. We tried various drugs to see which one would suit me. Some made me ill and others helped me through some awful panic attacks.The panic attacks for me were one of the worst aspects of the illness.

My psychiatrist told me that I was suffering 'a mother and a father of a depression'. He explained in simple language what was happening to my brain and how the right tablet would cure it. I became very dependent on him and grew to trust him totally.

The rest of the summer of '91 was hell. Everybody else was getting so much enjoyment out of my beautiful baby – laughing at his gurgles, cuddling him, caring for him. I used to stand at my bedroom window and pull back the curtains just a little bit. I'd see mums pushing prams and buggies in the sun, while I stood in my dressing-gown weeping.

The thought of suicide only once entered my mind. It was a strong enough thought to have stuck in my mind. I felt that maybe if I ended my life then everyone else could get on with theirs. But what stopped me from opening the jar of tablets and swallowing the lot was one picture. That was of David having a new mum and never remembering me. Selfish perhaps – survival more like.

My patience was running low. I'd had it with coping. I'd had it with being miserable all the time. I'd had it with seeing my baby grow and not being able to enjoy him. I'd had it with family, friends, doctors telling me I'd be better.

My psychiatrist saw my despair on one visit in September, six months after David was born. He came out with those magic words, 'Do you really want me to find you a bed in a hospital?' I answered 'yes please' through my sobs of relief and failure. The bed in the hospital would be my rock to crawl under, but my God what a failure I felt as a wife, a mother, a daughter, a sister, a friend, a teacher, a woman.

I never thought I'd see the day when I'd be 'committing myself', but that's what I did. In late September 1991 I signed myself in and was to spend until mid-November there.

For a lot of that hospital stay I cried and cried. I was heavily sedated and slept a lot. I could only just lift my head off the pillow to drink my juice at breakfast then slump back onto the pillow to sleep. I slept and cried. I cried and slept. All the time my psychiatrist tried to find a drug to suit me. He even got a second opinion.

In all those 43 days I saw my baby twice. Now the thought of that separation upsets me, but at the time I felt I'd nothing to offer him and he was better off without me. The only person I wanted to see was my husband.

One of my happier memories of my hospital stay, and there were few, relates to my father. For some reason his visits always left me with a sense of calm. One day he sat down beside me and wrote something on a piece of paper. He explained to me that in order for gold to become pure it has to pass through intense heat. Then it goes from 18ct to 24ct. He went on to say that my depression was like that fire and I'd come out the other end a 24ct mum. I was encouraged by that thought and perhaps that moment in time marks the turning point in my recovery. I still have the piece of paper, by the way.

Eventually a tablet that had been on the market for twenty years was the one that agreed with me. I can't begin to tell you how relieved I was. I was so afraid that I'd have to have ECT and scenes from *One Flew Over The Cuckoo's Nest* used to haunt me.

My path to recovery was slow. One doesn't recover overnight from PND. One day I was let out for a few hours. My spirits sank on returning and it was then I knew I was on the road to recovery.

If I said I was delighted to be discharged I would be lying. I was very nervous and apprehensive. I was still on a lot of medication and my legs were like jelly. I found it very scary going up and down stairs. I set myself a target of returning to work in January.

Christmas 1991 was bearable and I returned to work in January 1992. By June of that year, fifteen months after David's birth, I can say I was fully recovered.

Three years after David's birth I became pregnant again. On my first visit to my gynaecologist he suggested I make an appointment to see the newly appointed consultant psychiatrist at the Coombe Women's Hospital to talk through my first experience and set some plan in motion in the event of a re-occurrence.

A few days later I visited that psychiatrist and she listened and detailed my whole experience. She told me to feel free to call her if I ever felt the need to talk and to tell my husband he could do the same. She put a note on my hospital chart to be alerted the moment I went into labour. As I had decided not to breast feed I asked her to prescribe sleeping tablets for me while in the hospital.

I asked myself what could I do to make this pregnancy different from my last. My first resolution was to ensure that I avoided stressful situations at work. I took iron tablets and ate very healthily. I took plenty of rest and luckily I had the summer off before my baby was due.

I smile to myself when I think of the days that followed Stephen's birth. I had no visitors except family this time and I got plenty of rest. As each new day began and as my beautiful new baby was brought to me it began to dawn on me that PND wasn't presenting itself. The nurses reminded me that the psychiatrist was available to talk and I took the greatest of pleasure in telling them I didn't feel the need to see her.

My plan of campaign didn't end on leaving the hospital. When I settled the baby in I took all offers to help, especially when people offered to take my older child for a few hours. I took the phone off the hook every time Stephen slept and I slept as well. I put a note on the front door asking people not to ring the doorbell as there was a new baby in the house.

I even enjoyed the 4am feeds! Yes I know that's hard to believe. But you must remember that with each feed given and nappy changed and with each decision made I was regaining my much battered confidence in myself as a mum.

I remember one night picking Stephen out of the carrycot for his feed and a wave of very strong emotion engulfed me. I cuddled him close to me and it was as if we melted into one. The smell of him entered my heart and I knew I'd made it. This time I could enjoy it.

Tony

I met my wife Lorelle Turner in 1986 in Australia. The following year we married in her home town of Brisbane. By 1993 we had three beautiful children; two boys born in 1989 and 1991, and a little girl born in July.

Lorelle was a highly organised person. She adored travelling having visited fifty-one countries. She loved to try different things and enjoyed cooking and her numerous hobbies. After the birth of our first son in May 1989, Lorelle suffered from two weeks of depression ten weeks after the birth. This was treated very successfully with medication and she made a quick recovery.

Nine months after the birth of our second son in July 1991 Lorelle suffered three weeks of depression but she responded quickly to medication again and it passed.

The depression which set in after the birth of our daughter in July 1993 was more severe. It struck four months after the birth. Lorelle's symptoms were anxiety and an inability to sleep. She found herself unable to concentrate or make decisions, lost all her confidence and was simply unable to cope.

It was a vicious circle. She was unable to face meeting people and yet she badly needed to get out and about for a break. She improved after three months and in early 1994 seemed to be getting back to her old self.

In late February 1994 she had a relapse and all the symptoms returned. Within a few days, without any warning, my wife took an overdose of prescribed tablets and she died.

My whole world fell apart and I experienced so many feelings at the time. I felt totally inadequate at having been unable to help Lorelle. I also experienced much anger at the lack of expertise and information regarding PND. It is soul destroying to see a lovely person like my wife, so full of vitality, disintegrate before your eyes. I loved her dearly even when the stress on myself and the children at times seemed unbearable.

If I could start all over again there are certain things I would do differently. I certainly wouldn't hide my wife's illness from others. I would try to relieve the stress by getting people in to help with the housekeeping and the child minding. I would take regular breaks with my wife such as week-ends away to gain total rest. I would take control of all the tablets while at the same time keeping my wife's dignity. I would encourage some decision making because I feel doing everything for Lorelle was not a good idea in the long run.

I feel that there was very little mention of PND in the maternity hospital. Most babies are born in maternity hospitals and surely this is the most obvious place to issue information about PND to expectant women.

I wonder is it right that doctors prescribe and chemists supply a month's supply of lethal drugs to a person who is under such pressure and so vulnerable? Doctors should warn husbands and families about the dangerous nature of drugs in a depressed person's hands. One never thinks that one's own partner would contemplate anything so drastic.

I have to thank our families and friends, especially three women who were always there for us. My children and I are coping with our huge loss.

Ursula

I had never heard of PND until six years ago (July 10, 1989) when half way through a long labour I experienced a strange feeling of 'something leaving me.' After the birth I suppose on the outside I was like anybody just after a baby, but inside I was empty. I had just had a beautiful 10lb 6oz baby boy, Luke, and I didn't know what was wrong with me. I made one attempt to tell the doctor that something had gone 'terribly wrong' with my head. Alas, he dismissed it as a touch of the 'baby blues', 'you'll be fine when you get home'. But it wasn't to be.

After a few days at home with a husband who couldn't have

been better and a baby who slept most of the time, my mind was in a turmoil. I spent my days crying, not sleeping and felt totally detached from everything and everyone around me, including baby Luke. My GP was called and when the anti-depressants failed to work I ended up in a psychiatric hospital. That's where I spent a month of my life in August 1989. I had just had my first baby – he was twelve days old. My stay in that geriatric psychiatric hospital was horrific to say the least. Bars on the windows, bolts on the doors, a light shone into my eyes at night (to see if I was asleep they said) – stripped of all my dignity and treated as a bold child. Apart from being drugged up to my eyes most of the time, no doctor stopped to consider my physical condition at that time. A mother two weeks after giving birth, having just given up breastfeeding very quickly, and bleeding heavily. I suffered further because John was told to bring baby Luke to me twice a day, so I could feed and change him. I had to do this with old women looking on and clamouring to take him.

If my going into that hospital was traumatic, my coming home was even more so. Everybody thought that I was 'cured' and 'normal' again but of course I wasn't. John had had to look after Luke and organise household tasks while I was in hospital. I felt like an intruder in my own home. I couldn't bear to be on my own and would scream every time John left the room. Despite reassurances from John and my family I knew that there had to be help for me other than anti-depressants. There had to be other women suffering like me, who would understand what I was going through. After many phonecalls I finally got in touch with Bernie Brennan from the PND support group. She invited me to come along to their meeting in September 1989. I went there with mixed feelings, but any fears that I had were soon put to rest. I remember sitting at a table with six other women who asked if I would like to share my experience and this I did. At last there were other women like me and, more importantly, some of them had recovered from their ordeal. They didn't criticise or judge me.

Life was still pretty intolerable but knowing that next month would bring another meeting somehow kept me going. I also had plenty of women who kept in touch if I needed support.

After a few meetings I gradually found that I didn't talk about myself as much, that I was listening to others and even giving some reassurance to new mums.

I had a set-back in November 1989 when I foolishly took tablets. To this day I haven't really found the answer to this. All I now know is that I didn't want to die; it was a cry for help. In some ways it marked a turning point in my depression for me. The fact that I had survived meant so much. Finally in the New Year of 1990, the veil of darkness was lifting in my life, and I was coming out of the long tunnel of my depression. I did get better and had a baby girl, Rebecca, in November 1991 and no PND.

I have never looked back since.

John

Ursula and I were really looking forward to the birth of our first child.

Luke was born and I expected Ursula to be tired for a few days but she wasn't her usual bubbly self. When she and the baby came home I realised she was ill and definitely not well mentally. I was depending on her to show me how to feed, change, mind and care for the baby but she couldn't do it herself or show me. She appeared completely depressed, sleepless, anxious, unable to cope. Here was I minding a new baby about which I knew nothing, and a seriously ill wife. I certainly hadn't been prepared for this. I knew I needed medical help for Ursula and a crash course in babycare.

I called our GP. He said that Ursula had postnatal depression and prescribed anti-depressants. A few days passed and she was much worse. She was losing contact with reality, was hallucinating even. I called the GP again and he advised that we take her to a psychiatric hospital. Ursula agreed.

As I left her in the hospital looking completely lost and confused I felt so sad for her. As I was driving back home, new baby in the back of the car, I cried. I had just delivered my wife to a psychiatric hospital; for how long I did not know. She had looked forward so much to this time, to our new baby, and look at the mess we were in now. The psychiatrist assured me that she would recover but I didn't believe him. I saw a hospital full of seriously mentally ill patients and I didn't like it.

I got help. My family and Ursula's immediately sprung to the rescue offering advice and practical help. They offered to mind Luke but I wanted to and did mind him and keep him myself. I took him to the hospital twice daily. Ursula didn't begin to recover immediately. The hospital was a grim, Dickensian, cold place with bad smells, bad sounds, barred windows, old, geriatric and mentally ill patients, shuffling, shambling and muttering. However the nurses were excellent, gave me very good advice and counselling, and I saw her begin to recover.

She came home but was not fully recovered. Now came the really difficult time. She would have bouts of suspicion, depression, guilt, anger, and irrational behaviour which were often difficult to predict. I tried to allow her to be wife and mother, a role she had missed for the first six weeks of Luke's life, but I couldn't trust her. I didn't think she would hurt Luke or herself but I couldn't be sure. I went back to my work as a teacher. Ursula was still finding life difficult. I would be short-tempered with her at times, treat her like a child, be impatient

Through all this time I suffered headaches, worry, stress and tension. However I didn't become ill because I got good help and advice.

I saw Ursula gradually recovering. I saw a real breakthrough when she contacted other women who had recovered from postnatal depression. I got to believe she would recover when I contacted recovered women and their husbands.

Looking back over the whole episode there are changes I would make or would have liked. Starting with the maternity hospital; I would like more information at the pre-natal classes, and more advice on bringing the baby home. In our experience once the baby was born the hospital felt it had fulfilled its purpose. As regards the psychiatric hospital, it was not at all geared for PND.

There were no baby facilities or family facilities and very narrow and strict visiting hours not suitable for a newborn baby. A mother and baby unit would have helped Ursula to have a role as a mother, to have a relationship with her new baby, and would certainly have helped me.

There are things I have learned from all this. I have a stronger relationship with Ursula. We have battled on and succeeded together. My trust and confidence in her have not been misplaced. She made a complete recovery and we now have two lovely children.

Claire

I always wanted to have children. Having helped my mother rear my five step-sisters, I always yearned for children of my own. It was a dream come true when Paddy and I discovered we were about to become parents back in 1984. Over the moon would be an understatement. My pregnancy became a difficult one in the latter months. I put on a lot of weight and at 29 weeks had a haemorrhage. This resulted in a month's rest in hospital, three scans, and the knowledge that my baby would be born by caesarean section at 36 weeks. However, the baby had a mind of its own even then and I actually went into labour at 36 weeks. Thankfully I lived with my in-laws at the time and my mother-in-law was just a great support for me. Fifteen hours later, after much puffing and panting and trying to inhale gas at the right time, I gave birth to a beautiful girl, whom we called Louise.

Louise was perfect but as she weighed in at just 4lbs 11ozs, she was put in an incubator and kept at the nearest Paediatric Unit which was in Limerick, for a month. It was a long month. I visited her every day and bottle fed her. I hated being away from her. Thankfully she thrived and was soon settling into her new home in Ennistymon. Surplus weight disappeared and the episiotomy became just a bad memory as we became totally engrossed in our little bundle of joy. I couldn't believe a person could be so happy. Suddenly, my happiness ended with a bang. I woke up one night, about four months after she was born, and had the first of many panic attacks. I'd had a bad dream and I guess it brought it on. I went back to sleep hoping I'd be okay in the morning, but I wasn't.

I got more panicky as the week went by and began to fear I'd harm the baby. I was so afraid of what was happening, I told nobody in case Louise would be taken away from me and I'd be locked away. Eventually Paddy realised I wasn't myself and coaxed me to see a doctor. I was put on anti-depressants and advised to see a psychiatrist which I did and it all helped. After a few months the depression did go away but I wasn't really back to myself. I knew nothing about PND nor did I know of anyone who had been through it and recovered fully. I still felt overawed by it all and sort of isolated.

Then I became pregnant again and actually forgot about it for a while as I was in great form and suddenly decided that I'd accept I was better and not be upsetting myself wondering what had caused it. I was back working, my best friend was caring for Louise and everything was back to normal. Then, all of a sudden, I went into labour, this time at 31 weeks and 6 days into my pregnancy.

It took me a few hours to realise it was really happening and, after organising a baby-sitter for Louise, I raced to the hospital where 20 minutes later Patrick was born weighing all of 3lbs and 12ozs. I was convinced the child would die, he was so small. Again, he was whisked off to Limerick to the Paediatric Unit where he stayed for eight long weeks. While there, doctors discovered he had a reflex problem in his left kidney and they informed us that if it didn't clear up in a year he'd be heading to Crumlin for treatment. I had always associated the Children's Hospital in Crumlin with seriously ill children and my heart sank to my toes. The only light to shine was the fact that the problem wasn't a fatal one. While all this was going on, my dear mother-in-law was diagnosed with cancer and given weeks to live. The day after her operation, Patrick had been admitted for tests and the doctors allowed me to bring him to her part of the hospital so she could hug him. We didn't know if she'd be able to by the time his tests were finished.

Patrick finished his tests in mid-September and my mother-in-law died in late October. I went back to work in early November and when I got up that first morning to go to work I just knew the depression was coming back, and I was right. As November drifted into December, the panic attacks and fears came back. I tried to keep going, hoping it would go away of its own accord. I felt by not admitting to having it, it might just vanish. How silly I was. I got worse and worse. I felt totally alone in the world. I figured nobody else could get like this and that I must be a freak of nature. After six months I went to my GP. He prescribed treatment and was very supportive. I hated having to take tablets. I had to try three different types before they had any effect, but all this time I yearned for information on PND, yearned to contact someone who really knew what was going on in my mind. I cried buckets of tears. They would stream down my face as I spoon fed the baby.

I'd take Louise up in my lap and hug her and wonder how in God's name I'd have a fear of harming her and Patrick. I really thought I should kill myself and give Paddy a chance to find a 'right' mother for them. Thankfully, I was too much of a coward to take my own life. But I felt so dead inside. It was like living in a dark tunnel with no sign of a light at the end. Looking back, I think my husband deserves to be a candidate for sainthood because he suffered too. He didn't know what was causing this and I think he blamed himself at times, wondering what could have brought it on.

Well, 1986 was a long dark year but sometime in August of that year I read about a support group for PND sufferers in London. I put pen to paper straight away and poured my heart out to them. They put me in touch with a former sufferer who wrote to me constantly and, at last, the feeling of isolation disappeared and a light appeared at the end of the tunnel. I read and re-read her letters. They were better than any anti-depressant to me. An improvement came on me straight away and just having contact with someone who'd been there and recovered and knew and understood made me feel 'normal' again.

The PND group also sent me leaflets on PND and kept up contact with me. Learning about PND and the many things which cause it was fantastic. I began to realise I was one of many going through this awful illness and that, most importantly of all, it would go away. Mind you, it did not go away overnight; it phased itself out. At times I would still get panic attacks, especially when my period was due, but even though they were horrible, I'd calm down a lot quicker and tell myself it was one less attack to go before recovery. I also bought a book by Dr Claire Weekes called *More Self Help For Your Nerves*. From reading it I got a full grasp on how I'd become so ill and also I taught myself how to overcome the panic attacks. Her book brought me to a 100% recovery.

While recovering, I promised myself that some day I'd try and help others, just like Adele (my volunteer) helped me. She continues to be my pen-pal and good friend. Well, with the help of a woman called Bernie Brennan, one of the co-founders of the *Postnatal Distress Association of Ireland* (see p. 88) support group, I set up *Mothers to Mothers Pen Pal Support* (see p. 87). I try to get former sufferers to write to those suffering now and to try to help them to recover. The most fulfilling thing is when these mothers write back to me and tell me how they've got better and thank me for my help. It makes it all worthwhile. Contact with former sufferers is a godsend. *Mothers to Mothers* is there for people who may not want to go to meetings or who may not have a support group in their locality. I also take calls on the phone as I feel a phone call can prevent a suicide. To those of you who read my story I say if you need help, or would like to help other sufferers, please write to me. (See p. 87 for address).

The happy ending to my story is that I became pregnant again in 1987. Of course I dreaded getting ill again. However I enjoyed my pregnancy, went full term and had a 7lb 5oz baby girl, Margaret. I was able to bring her home with me and apart from the initial four day baby blues I escaped the trauma of PND. I must also add that Patrick did in fact have to go to Crumlin for treatment over a three year period. He is now in perfect health and nobody would believe he was a mere 3lbs at birth.

Madge

I was seven days overdue, went in on a false alarm and was induced. It was the worst day of my life. I had been getting pains on and off for a few weeks before and went quickly into the third stage of labour. It was very busy in the labour ward and none of the nurses would believe me that things were so advanced after only being on the drip a short while. It took an hour from when the drip went in until my baby was born and I barely made it on to the table. I had intended to have an epidural but everything went so fast that it was not possible. Apparently two or three women in a thousand give birth this quickly after the drip. It was the most terrifying experience. I wished I was dead. My poor body really got a shock.

After delivery there was a change of shift. I was left in a room off the delivery room and they forgot about me for an hour. They took my baby away as he was in real distress and they just let us look at him for two seconds and whipped him off. He was born at 1pm and, despite asking several times, I didn't get him again until 9pm, eight hours later. I was really worried that he was handicapped. There was no bed on the delivery ward so I was downstairs in a gynaecological ward. I didn't want to be a nuisance. My husband went home at 5pm but before he went I sent him up to make sure our baby was OK. They said he was asleep and was all right, but didn't let him see him. I was not really convinced.

After this I was in great form and on a bit of a high. Nothing was too much trouble. I was just happy to have survived the birth! I breast fed the baby, same as my first, and everything went fine until the christening six weeks later. I got over tired having held it in the house. I thought I had lots of help but of course I did too much. The first night I got no sleep. Next the eating went and I couldn't cope with even small things. I kept thinking if I could only sleep I would be OK. But the most sleep I got was until 4am, when I awoke with my head spinning. I had all these thoughts that everything was my fault. I felt as though I was in a really dark tunnel. A week later I decided I needed help when I felt what was the point and life wasn't worth living. I did not have a clue where to go for help and rang a friend. We looked at all the options. I knew I must have PND even though I had never heard about it from my antenatal teacher or gynaecologist. I went to my GP who put me on anti-depressants.

For the next six months he juggled around with anti-depressants and relaxants. I was up and down like a yo yo. My family were going through hell every bit as much, if not more, than I was. It was a nightmare. We had no extended family and I felt so isolated. My friends were sick of listening and really did not understand. My parents were at their wit's end and couldn't understand why I couldn't pull myself together. 'Hadn't I a lovely home, beautiful children, good husband, good job etc...'.

Meanwhile I was going through hell, the days were so long and the decisions so big (what to wear, what to do for dinner). I dreaded the nights when I couldn't sleep and had all these thoughts racing around my head. I felt so much guilt and self-recrimination. My husband went through his own hell, watching me change into some sort of monster. When I was up I was so self-righteous and obnoxious, when down indecisive, whining and suicidal. I took a lot of anger out on my older child which was so unfair. I just wanted it all to end; the racing thoughts, the emptiness, the darkness, the pain and most of all the distress I was causing my husband and children. I thought – or knew – that they would be better off without me. I remember going to the GP one Saturday with my husband and children and feeling so bad that I hoped that he would put me in hospital where someone would look after me and keep me safe. He said the only place I could go was a psychiatric hospital. I nearly died of shock. So home we went for another weekend of hell. We were six months down the road at this stage. I asked to be sent to a psychiatrist and for the next two months I really tried to stay out of hospital. I pleaded with everyone – my GP, my psychiatrist, and my friends – to find someone who had experienced and recovered from PND and who would be willing to talk to me even just on the phone. I really felt I needed reassurance that I wasn't going mad and I would recover. It wasn't enough the professionals telling me, for that was their job. I kept asking if there was any sort of support group anywhere. Everytime the answers came back No, Sorry, Be patient, You will get better, Take your tablets. I didn't believe them.

Christmas was horrific that year. I barely remember Christmas day which was a disaster, although I really tried for the sake of the family. By January we were at breaking point and I was on the verge of a nervous breakdown. My two children were farmed out to a baby minder during the day and I was left on my own in the house, trying to fill the day. In hindsight we saw that was the worst thing as I had too much time to think and things really went crazy. During all this time my husband got no advice. He felt so helpless and really didn't know where to turn or what to do for the best.

I will never forget the day I ended up in the psychiatric hospital. To say it was a horrific experience is putting it mildly. It is hard to describe the terror a distressed mother feels when confronted by one of these places and separated from her baby. It was bad enough feeling as bad as I did without this added terror. The state of the building alone would depress the most sane. I was treated like someone without a brain. My confidence, the little I had left, went down the drain. I felt so isolated as there was no other woman there with PND. I only got to see my baby at weekends and sometimes it was hard to believe I even had him. If I was any bit emotional on Fridays they would not allow me out for weekends. This was a terrible torture and after it happened once I made sure there wasn't a re-occurence. While inside, very few people visited as they were terrified of the place and I couldn't blame them. My poor husband visited every day and I had an odd visit from my family.

I really fought hard to get out but it took six weeks, the longest weeks of my life. It took me another six months to get some of my confidence back. After coming out of hospital I got the address of the PND group in Dublin but it took me ages to write. I just wasn't able. It was sad that ten months of my life of hell had gone by at that stage. It was the longest and worst year of my life and I vowed if I ever got well I would be there for other sufferers. My illness went the long way around. I was unlucky .

The good thing is that I got better and in some weird way it has made me a better person, but I would not wish it on my worst enemy. My greatest frustration was at the lack of a support system. The public health nurse didn't even call once in the twelve months. I was also upset by the huge stigma involved. Former friends crossed the street to avoid me.

Anne

I write this with a different perspective from that which I had when I first wrote about my experience five years after the event. Now, eleven years distanced from my bout of postnatal depression the advantage I find is that I am less angry and passionate about the whole experience, the disadvantage being that my recollection of different details may not be as good.

I married relatively late in life, in my early thirties. We were both keen to have children so I became pregnant within our first year of marriage and we both looked forward with great joy to the birth of our first child. My pregnancy was relatively straightforward, apart from twenty-four hours a day 'morning sickness' and severe colic during the first four months. I attended the usual antenatal classes for first-time mothers, became determined to have the most natural childbirth possible (birthing chair and no drugs!!) and to breastfeed my baby. Looking back I think this reflected a perfectionist part of my personality that was to be one of the factors pre-disposing me to PND. Like a lot of women expecting their first child I was also big into books about pregnancy and child-rearing and these and a general ignorance of babies (I was the youngest in my family) led to fairly unrealistic expectations of the joys of motherhood and babyhood.

Looking back, another pre-disposing factor was that I had only moved into the area where we lived about a year before the baby was due. I was out working every day and didn't really know the people around me. Where I lived was also a considerable distance from my close friends, two of whom were also pregnant at the time, so I felt relatively isolated.

I should like to say at this point that postnatal depression was never mentioned in my ante-classes and that I personally had never heard of it. In my pregnancy book I never actually read beyond the birth sections and even if I had done so, ten lines on the 'baby blues' and three quarters of a page on 'puerperal psychosis' (out of a total of 575 pages) was hardly what you call eye-catching or attention grabbing!

Far from a natural birth, I ended up ten days over-due and haemorrhaging, before going to the maternity hospital, having a highly technological labour (monitors hooked to baby and me, inducing drips, etc) and a delivery that was so awful that the senior of the three midwives present (along with the senior houseman and eventually two paediatricians – quite a crowd!) sympathetically entreated me not to let it put me off having more children!

My baby, a boy, was in severe distress by the time he was born and was whisked away, with little or no explanation, by the paediatricians, to the special unit for sick babies. I was never really to find out, despite a few valiant efforts, what exactly was the problem. I relate all these details because I feel very strongly that my complete lack of control in the above scenario was one of the most critical factors in my subsequent decline into depression.

My anxiety over my baby's health and my total exhaustion after the birth, led paradoxically to an inability to relax and rest for the next few days and starting breastfeeding led to interrupted sleep as well.

I came home, thrilled with my baby but very, very tired. My mother had died four years previously and I had no female relatives of my own close by, so a relative of my husband kindly offered to come and stay for the first week I was home. Unfortunately she had considerable experience of babies and children and, quite unintentionally, made me feel very inadequate as a mother and once again took control of events away from me.

I had to bring my son back to the clinic two weeks after coming home to be checked out (no, I wasn't told why) and it was at this point, three weeks after giving birth, that postnatal depression kicked in.

I never realised I was depressed because my initial symptoms were anxiety and irritability. I began to lose my sleep pattern. It was my inability to sleep that brought me to my GP. He mentioned depression and prescribed anti-depressants and tranquillisers (afterwards when I started to educate myself about PND I was to feel aghast at the lack of logic of this combination). He said I would feel better in about 10 days. I didn't and I was very anxious about taking drugs while I was breastfeeding so I stopped taking them. My depression deepened. My confidence disappeared and my self-esteem plummeted. Pressurised by well-meaning relatives and friends I decided exhaustion due to breastfeeding was the root of my problems and despite having been relatively successful at it, I stopped. I think this was the 'body-blow'. Psychologically it was so bad for me that I became suicidal. In an oddly calm and, to myself, quite rational way, I decided I was such a bad mother that my baby and husband would both be much better off if I was gone, permanently. I picked my night (my husband was due to go out to a meeting) and my method (an overdose). I made up bottles for the following 24 hours, calmly wiped all the kitchen surfaces with Milton and decided that there would be no note – for everyone's sake they had to think it was accidental, that I hadn't meant it and, especially, that it wasn't something that was their fault. Bear in mind that neither my husband nor myself really felt I was depressed – we were both still seeing it as exhaustion and inexperience with babies.

Fortunately for me – thought I didn't feel so that night – my husband's meeting was cancelled and he returned early preventing me from completing my desperate plans.

He insisted I see a psychiatrist – a woman – whom he knew and she immediately hospitalised me.

I still didn't accept the fact that I was depressed and felt a total fraud in a psychiatric ward full of people who had 'real' reasons for being depressed. Like myself, most people had never heard of postnatal depression and they couldn't empathise with the fact that having a baby – a normally joyful event – could lead to depression.

I didn't like being in that hospital separated from my baby who was being cared for by relations, nor did I like being treated like a child myself, by the psychiatric nurses. Fortunately, my psychiatrist – later to do the first significant piece of Irish research and publication about PND – was excellent and so was her boss. Between them they found the right medication for me and talked to me and counselled me and I gradually began to get better.

Seven weeks later I went home. I had been home for days and weekends prior to that and had looked after my son in so far as I could on those occasions, so that after I came home I started to look after him full time. It was difficult – my self-esteem and confidence were still way below normal. My friends who had been pregnant had had their babies and were coping marvellously and I envied them from the bottom of my heart.

I saw my psychiatrist on a regular basis, returning to work when my baby was five months old. I was horrified to find that my confidence in that area was pretty abysmal too – I had thought it was all baby-related, but postnatal depression is the same as any depression in the lowering of self-esteem and loss of self-confidence. Eight months down the line I really was getting back to myself and at nine months was weaned off my medication. I'd say I wasn't fully myself until my son was a year old.

All this time I met only one other person with a condition similar to mine – another woman in the hospital who had puerperal psychosis and who was so ill that she was in no position to talk to me about it. Only one friend had come across it – her sister had suffered from it years before. There was total ignorance about it. I was quite open about my illness – all my friends, relatives and colleagues at work knew about it but the ignorance of its general existence was almost total. I got on with my life. We decided to have another child but were hedging our bets and leaving a four year gap. However, having given up the pill because I found it tended to be depressive (I certainly recognised the condition now!) and resorted to natural family planning, we got pregnant a year early!

This time around we were prepared. I knew the realities of motherhood and babyhood. I had gotten involved in my local community and so didn't feel as isolated. I was also determined that I was going to be in control of this birth and assert myself in a major league way in the maternity hospital – and I did! Looking from the outside, this was the baby I should have got PND on. After a relatively easy birth and safe delivery of a healthy second son, somehow he had a brain haemorrhage in the hours after birth, nearly died, was considered a possibility for brain and physical handicap but fortunately recovered and at eighteen months was pronounced perfectly 'normal'. In all that time I wasn't depressed for a second – worried, desperately so at times, but not depressed. It was to be another two years before I saw an article about PND in *The Irish Times* and joined the woman in that article in forming a support group for women who had PND.

What a relief and what a joy it was to meet other people who had experienced – and in many cases in those early days were still experiencing – PND! I had always felt such a freak when I was suffering from PND. It would have been great to know I wasn't as alone as I thought. If there had been a support group I might never have become as ill as I did or for as long as I did. I need never have been hospitalised or separated from my baby. No psychiatrist, no nurse, no GP can ever possibly understand and empathise with a PND sufferer in the way others who have been through the same experience can.

My involvement with the support group and with the Postnatal Distress Association of Ireland over the following years has been one of the most satisfying parts of my life and I hope more people who have suffered PND, especially those whose recovery has been speeded along due to the support of other sufferers, will become involved as supporters themselves and help to destigmatise the illness and increase public awareness of it.

Fiona

When I look at my daughter now, I find it hard to believe that twelve months ago I thought my world had come to an end.

Myself and my husband had been married for six years when my daughter was born. After the first year of marriage an unplanned pregnancy ended in a miscarriage at eleven weeks. We decided to continue on as before and think about children again sometime in the future. I found it difficult to continue as before but nonetheless it was three years later before we decided to start a family. After a year and a half of trying for a baby, I was over the moon when I discovered I was pregnant. I had a wonderful pregnancy. I felt so healthy and happy and my family and friends told me how well I looked all through the nine months. We prepared the spare room for the baby and when I went into labour two days after my due date, we knew we were ready.

My daughter was born after a five hour labour and as she had some fluid on her lung she was taken straight to intensive care. I remember feeling utterly exhausted and somewhat indifferent to the fact that I did not have my new baby with me when I was brought to my room. While in hospital I felt so tired I found it hard to image how I was going to cope once I went home. Women who had had such long and difficult labours seemed to be 'up and about' within twenty-four hours. They all seemed so happy and looking forward to going home with their new babies. Though I was afraid of going home, I was not enjoying my hospital stay either. I was so tired and people kept on visiting me. Why wouldn't they just stay away and let me rest! If only I could get some sleep I would be fine!

Once home I quickly realised that things were not as they should be. I was struggling day after day with feelings of total despair at the situation in which I found myself. My daughter did not sleep through the night as we had hoped and I remember sitting at the top of the stairs on many a night, rocking my baby in my arms, tears streaming down my face, feeling sick and panicking as to how I was going to get through the next day. My husband had returned to work and was unable to get any more time off.

He would get up at 6.00 a.m. and take the baby until 8.00 a.m. and would then go to work. He would then come home at lunch time to try and sort out whatever crisis was happening. Each day I drove to my mother's, handed my daughter over to her and went to bed for a couple of hours in the afternoon. My husband's parents took my baby on a number of occasions to give me a few hours to myself. There are not many new mothers who have had as much help as I did and yet I could not stop feeling exhausted and desperately unhappy.

I was beginning to dread being alone with my daughter in the house. What if she started to cry and I couldn't stop her. My husband was angry with me for not taking the phone off the hook and for running to the front door every time the bell rang. He didn't understand. If I cut myself off from the outside world how was I going to be rescued? Each time the phone rang or someone came to the door, I thought this is it, this is the person who is going to save me. It never was.

By the end of the fourth week at home things were really falling apart. I was constantly asking my friends who had children if they had felt like this after they had their babies. I knew by their replies that they had not. I was unable to make a decision about anything to do with my daughter without looking up books or ringing my mother, my friends, or the district nurse.

My husband's parents had organised a family dinner to celebrate the birth of their new grandchild. Everyone was looking forward to it except for me. I thought if I went to bed for a couple of hours before we left, I would be able to cope once we got there. I lay on the bed and cried. My sister by chance rang from overseas to see how I was and I found myself telling her how I had to go to this dinner and how I did not know how I was going to get through it. My sister persuaded me that not only should I not go to dinner but that I should talk to my husband and explain to him exactly how I was feeling. After a long talk with my husband we agreed that I should go and see a doctor and seek some help. This was the turning point for me.

My mother-in-law had recommended her GP and I made an appointment. I spoke to her at some length and she asked me a number of questions. It was so nice to speak to someone who was not telling me that 'all first time mothers feel like this'. She explained the difference between the so called 'baby blues' and postnatal depression and told me that I was in fact suffering from the latter. As well as putting me on medication, she gave me some practical advice, such as doing something with my husband which was just for the two of us and nothing to do with the baby, and making sure that I got out for a walk each day to work off some of the adrenaline which had built up, no matter how tired I felt. The medication she put me on at night gave me a restful night's sleep for the first time since my baby had been born.

Gradually things started to improve. It certainly did not change overnight but I was beginning to see some light at the end of the tunnel. The fact that the awful despair and helplessness I had been feeling had been acknowledged by my doctor as something which was out of my control and was not something which 'all new mothers felt so just get on with it' was indeed the first step to my recovery. It was also so encouraging to be told that this was something which would not last forever and that there were steps which I could take myself to aid my own recovery. At first a number of these steps seemed selfish to me, but I soon discovered that by saying 'thank you very much for the invitation but I do not feel up to it at present', I was not in fact offending people, who were after all my friends and family and therefore understood the reasons for my refusals.

Looking back now it all seems like a bad dream and yet I have learned a lot from the experience. I certainly know my limitations and I will always appreciate the help and support I was given by my husband, my family and friends. As for my daughter, despite the rocky start, I don't think I could adequately express the joy she has brought into our lives in the twelve short months she has been with us.

Coping with Postnatal Depression

i) Dos and Don'ts

Do:

• Talk to your doctor about any anxieties and worries you may have during your pregnancy. It helps no-one to bottle up your fears.

• Attend your pre-natal classes.

• Discuss with your partner how a new baby in the home will change your lives. Discuss what you think will change and how best to deal with this change.

• Try to avoid major upheavals coming up to, or immediately after the birth, e.g. moving house, changing job.

• Tell someone in the hospital if you feel low or abnormally high after the birth.

• Take plenty of rest while in hospital by limiting visitors to a minimum.

• Accept a visit from the hospital psychiatrist if offered.

• Accept genuine offers of help when you return home. Let family and friends help with the household chores of cooking and cleaning as long as the result is that you rest. This doesn't mean that you can't cope, but that you are taking a back seat for a few weeks.

• Let your partner see how much work is involved in caring for a new baby. Let him change nappies, give feeds, make bottles.

He needs to feel involved even if you don't think he's doing as good a job as you!

• Make it your business to get to know your Public Health Nurse and visit your baby clinic and let them and your doctor know of any worries or anxieties you may have. If you find this difficult, bring your partner or friend along with you for support.

• Join a mother and toddlers group.

• Take time out for yourself. When the baby sleeps, you try to rest as well. Be practical. Take the phone off the hook, even put a note on the front door asking not to be disturbed. Even if you don't sleep, relaxing will help you in your recovery.

• Make time for your partner. Get a baby-sitter and go out together. It can be something simple like going for a walk or taking a drive. Use this time to relax and forget the stresses at home.

• Try to include other children you may have in helping with the new baby. Like your partner they too need to feel included.

• Eat properly. Try to avoid 'snacking' on coffee and chocolate. Stick to a good balanced diet. Avoid 'junk food'.

• Take care of yourself. Make sure you are doing as much as possible to mind your health. Try to get in a little exercise each day and perhaps listen to relaxing music for a few minutes.

• Take your medication as prescribed. Remember anti-depressants are there to help you recover. You won't become addicted to anti-depressants.

• Attend self help meetings in your area. Contact PNDAI (address on p. 88).

• Get your illness explained to you. You will find that this will help lift the guilt you may be feeling.

• Accept your depression. Try to avoid seeking an instant recovery. This tends to lead to more anxiety and depression. Be as patient as you can in these awful circumstances.

• Tell someone who won't judge you if you have obsessive thoughts or if you think about harming yourself or the baby.

• Write down your feelings.

• Remember that however important your job may seem, you must face the fact that you cannot work if you are ill. You must wait until you feel ready to cope with this particular pressure.

Don't

• Don't be afraid to tell the nurses and doctors that you feel low or high while in hospital. If you have had a bad birth experience, tell them.

• Don't hide your illness from friends and family. There is no need to feel ashamed of having PND. They are there to help and support you through this crisis.

• Don't try to be Superwoman. Try to do one chore per day when you feel up to it, and don't be hard on yourself if you don't manage to do it. Delegate the rest.

• Don't entertain visitors who require work. Anyone who visits you should be prepared to make the tea, wash up and most importantly lend a sympathetic ear to your problems.

• Don't be afraid to talk to your doctor about the side effects of any medication you may be on.

• Don't be afraid to change your doctor if you are not happy with the advice you are being offered.

• Don't rule out psychiatric help if it is suggested to you. Many sufferers find the combination of drugs and psychiatric help to be the turning point in their illness.

• Don't eat junk food. Increase your intake of fresh fruit and vegetables.

• Don't ignore your feelings. If you feel like expressing your anger in a physical way the first thing is to ensure your children are in a safe place. Then you can scream, cry, pound a pillow, tear up a magazine, get into the shower and let the water wash away your anger. When you have released your anger calm down by having a cup of tea or listening to some soothing music.

• Don't be afraid to cry. It is a good way to release tensions and again it doesn't mean you are unable to cope.

• Don't feel you are alone. There are many women out there feeling the way you feel today. The last thing you must do is to suffer in silence. Always remember there is help at PNDAI (see p. 88).

In short ...

A new mother needs:

- Rest
- Peace
- Care
- Support
- Pampering
- Nurturing
- Mothering

ii) Dealing with panic attacks

For many women suffering with PND one of the most frightening experiences is a panic attack. If a woman can recognise the early signs of an attack and apply relaxation techniques, she will find that gradually she will be able to cope with the attacks, and slowly they will diminish both in frequency and severity.

What is a panic attack?

Many events in life cause us to feel stressed. Obvious examples are bereavement, birth of a baby, exams, job loss, marriage, flying etc. There is no end to the list of what people find stressful. What one person might consider stressful may not bother another. When we are stressed we release hormones into our bodies. These are adrenaline and noradrenaline. We may know them as flight and fight hormones.

What these hormones do is:

- make our hearts beat faster
- make us breathe more quickly
- slow down our digestive process
- tense our muscles.

In other words they get our bodies ready for potentially life – threatening situations. For example, athletes deliberately 'psyche' themselves up before a race to help them to perform better. Once the race is over the level of stress hormones will revert to normal.

This reaction is not appropriate for a new mother when she finds herself in a situation where it is obvious she can't fight or flee – at a check-out counter for example or when dealing with a crying baby. So the stress hormones keep pumping into the body and the end result is a panic attack.

The symptoms of a panic attack include:

- palpitations (rapid heart beat)
- experiencing difficulty in breathing
- feeling nauseous

- fear
- dizziness
- sweating
- trembling.

The main reason for many of the above symptoms is hyperventilation where a woman is breathing very quickly. Breathing into a paper bag or into cupped hands, to re-breathe her own breath, will help overcome the attack.

It is very important to deal with panic attacks as, eventually, if left untreated, the very idea of a panic attack may bring on an attack.

How can panic attacks be prevented?

Once you clearly understand what is happening some of the fear will go away. Learning deep breathing and relaxation techniques is the next obvious step.

Try to breathe in slowly through your nose, hold for five seconds and exhale very slowly through your mouth. Repeat ten times. Also try to relax your muscles starting from the neck and working your way down to your toes.

Once you learn these deep breathing and relaxation techniques you can apply them when you feel an attack coming on.

Panic attacks are terrifying and it is impossible to make those around understand what you are panicking about, but remember, a panic attack won't kill you.

iii) Advice for Carers:

The partner:

• The most important fact to understand is that PND is an illness. It is nobody's fault and your partner is not 'putting it on'. It is a serious illness and must be taken seriously. You have to accept your partner's depression. Don't try to push it away or run away from it by belittling it or denying that it exists. Your partner is not 'mad'.

• There is no point in telling her to pull herself together – she is incapable of doing so.

• There are many things you can do to help by reducing all sources of stress in her life.

• Let her express her feelings and when she does, don't dismiss them no matter how silly they may seem. To her these fears are very real.

• Try to build up her confidence by showing her consideration and sympathy.

• Praise her for anything she does manage to achieve in the day.

• Don't try to reason with her. PND sufferers find it difficult to think logically.

• Protect her from too many visitors and from criticism from friends and relations.

• Don't let her feel guilty.

• No matter how hard it may be, try to be patient.

• Don't let her feel guilty about her inability to cope, her unkempt appearance, her unfinished jobs.

• Pull your weight where household chores are concerned. Help with the cooking, ironing, feeding, etc.

• Ensure she gets a break, even for a couple of hours, to do something for herself.

• Try to encourage her to socialise while remembering that she may find dealing with crowds stressful and frightening.

• Get a baby-sitter and spend some time together away from the baby.

• Share the night feeds, at weekends, if you are working. Sleep is essential on the road to making a positive recovery.

• Make sure she is eating properly. Women with PND need to have three nutritious meals a day. She mustn't binge on junk food.

• Attend self-help meetings with her if she asks you to.

• If she has 'gone off' the idea of sex don't pressure her. You must show patience and understanding. Loss of libido is a symptom of PND and not a reflection on your relationship. Hold her hand, hug her, offer her a shoulder to cry on.

• If the doctor has prescribed tablets, make sure she takes them. They will help her to get well.

• Don't suffer in silence. Explain the illness to your families. Encourage them to contact their GPs or PNDAI (see p. 88) to get information on the illness.

• Confide in a friend or phone PNDAI (see p. 88).

• No matter what she says don't show shock.

• If she is low, try to ensure she is not left alone.

Finally remember that she is still your wife or girlfriend and that this awful nightmare will end. She will begin to take control of her life again. She will be able to return to work and look after you and the children. Your reactive depression will lift as she begins to relax and laugh and you both will make a full recovery. Many couples have found that surviving PND together has strengthened their relationship, bringing them closer together.

Family and Friends:

You can be of help in two ways. You can offer practical assistance and you can be supportive.

Practical Assistance:

• Take the baby for a few hours to let the mum have a break. Make sure that this separation from the baby does not cause her anxiety.

• You could cook some meals, have her and her partner for dinner, and fill her freezer with ready made dinners.

• Even if she has the use of a car, offer her lifts.

• Help with the household chores. You could offer to do the ironing or washing up or do the shopping.

• Take the other children so she can have time alone with the baby.

• Go with her to self-help group meetings.

• Baby-sit so she and her partner can go out for a couple of hours.

Ways of being supportive:

• Listen. Careful and sympathetic listening will help you to understand the problem better and will have a healing effect on the PND sufferer.

• If she is suicidal or mentions wanting to harm herself or the baby, strongly suggest she seeks professional help.

• Don't express shock at anything she may say.

• Avoid blaming her partner for problems or creating bad feeling between the couple.

• Don't tell her to 'buck up' and feel lucky that she has such a healthy baby, etc. This only adds to the guilt.

• Encourage her to contact you at any time.

Remember she will get better. With your patience and understanding her recovery will be made easier and quicker.
Things will return to normal.

iv) Where to turn to for help

Different women respond to different treatments in different ways. What might help in the recovery process of one woman may be of no value to another. Here are suggested avenues of help to explore. You may find one suggestion may help or indeed a combination of many.

Keep searching until you find the one for you.

Find someone sympathetic to talk to, someone who understands your anxieties without judging you. An obvious person would be a member of PNDAI. They operate a help line which is answered by recovered mothers. They also have self-help meetings around the country where you can go and express your worries and fears in complete confidentiality. They welcome partners, family members and friends to come along. All details of the meetings can be obtained by phoning PNDAI (see p. 88)

Call your maternity hospital if you feel depressed or manic when you return home. You will find a list of maternity hospitals and their guidelines on dealing with PND in Appendix II. Remember they cannot help you if you don't let them know you're suffering.

Visit your GP. Don't feel a failure if you have to admit to being unable to cope. GPs see plenty of women with PND come through their doors so you needn't feel you are a 'freak'. Your doctor will assess your needs and suggest a remedy. She may or may not prescribe anti-depressants. If she does, be sure to ask about side effects. Don't be afraid to take them as anti-depressants are non-addictive. If you are not happy with the response you get from your GP, find one who will treat your illness with the seriousness it deserves.

You may need to see a psychiatrist to help you recover. Again don't shy away from this suggestion. If you had any other serious illness you would go and see a specialist to deal with it. So why treat your depressive illness any differently? Psychiatrists are trained to deal with depression. They won't judge you, but will suggest ways of helping you deal with your illness. If you are frightened at the thought of visiting a psychiatrist bring your partner or friend along to reassure you. If the psychiatrist suggests that you be hospitalised, don't panic. It is for your own good. It will take you away from a stressful situation and give you time to work through what is happening to you.

Consult a trained analyst such as a counsellor or psychologist whose method of work is non-directional.

Talk to your public health nurse when she comes to visit or when you go to the baby clinic. She shouldn't be surprised at seeing a mother in distress as 15% of all mothers get PND in some shape or form. She may have helpful suggestions on how to cope and relieve your anxieties.

Contact local women's groups such as *Irish Childbirth Trust* (*Cuidiú*) (see p. 86), or mother and toddler group. Meeting other mothers, and seeing that they too have worries and anxieties, can be of enormous value. It can also ease your sense of loneliness.

Find out if there is a *Community Mothers Scheme* running in your area and make contact with your local visitor. They provide a listening ear and great practical support to new mothers.

Contact the *Mothers to Mothers* pen-pal organisation (see p. 87). This service was set up by Claire O'Dwyer, herself a recovered PND sufferer. She will put you in touch with a recovered mum who will write to you while you continue to recover. This service will be of particular help to women who do not have access to self-help meetings.

Try relaxation techniques. There are many varieties of relaxation methods worth exploring:

- Yoga
- Relaxation tapes
- Homeopathy
- Reflexology
- Massage
- Aromatherapy

Get some exercise. This doesn't mean a ten mile jog every day. It could be something as simple as a 20 minute walk when your partner comes home in the evening, or a walk with the baby in the pram during the day. Exercise really does help in lifting depression and many GPs are prescribing it as part of helping those who suffer with depression.

Read up on your illness. If you understand it this will help take away some of the guilt you may be feeling.

Remember you will get better. I know it is hard to believe but have the patience to see it through. There is light at the end of the tunnel.

Self-help Groups and PND

The role of the self-help group in PND

Jane Fry

'After we have given birth it is as if we wake up to discover that a mountain of sand has been deposited in front of the door of our home. Some women get to work energetically to dig routes out. They have friends who come along and help. They work round the sand and over the sand: They find marvellously inventive ways to cope with the situation. Some women find one difficult route out and stick to that. Some try to dig a way through and get buried, others just look at it, feel defeated, retreat within their four walls and give up.' (Vivienne Welburn, *Postnatal Depression*, Fontana Original, 1980)

Whenever I have quoted these words to mothers, they have struck a chord. Becoming a mother is always a challenge but individual experiences are very varied and Vivienne Welburn's words capture well the spectrum of challenges involved. Members of PNDAI have had more difficulty than most mothers with their piles of sand and they have explored numerous ways of digging. They are now committed to encouraging other women as they dig, and as they search for answers to the many questions that postnatal distress raises: Where does the sand come from? How can it be prevented from piling up? Why do some women have enormous piles of wet coarse sand which get heavier and more compact by the day, whilst others have small dry piles of fine dry sand which seemingly disperse quite easily? What is the most efficient way to dig? Who can provide the shovels?

Of course members of PNDAI are not the only people trying to find answers to these questions but it is well established that a self-help group has an important role in stimulating interest in specific minority group issues and increasing awareness amongst professionals and the public. The work of self-help groups complements professional services and family support and they have become a major mental health resource. Research has generally allayed the fears of those professionals who were sceptical of self-help groups – some feeling that they promoted escapism and pathological dependence, or unnecessary isolation of stigmatised populations – and some of course feeling threatened by the perceived challenge to medical authority. Experience has also dimmed the romantic or zealous view of many who hailed the self-help group as a panacea for all human suffering. It is accepted that they are not for everyone and that they have their limits, but they have an important role to play and have become increasingly well integrated into community services in recent years. Political, economic and social influences have all played a part in this development.

Our aspirations for health care generally far outweigh the available resources, and self-help groups are very cost effective, relying as most do on goodwill and voluntary effort and very modest grants or funding. The impact of social change on mental health has been very significant and as traditional support networks have been eroded, strengthening the social networks to which people belong has become a priority. There has been a strong move away from centralised and institutionalised services towards the provision of a comprehensive range of accessible community based supports, with a greater focus on prevention, education and information. Self-help groups fit very neatly into this model of care, but they are also very popular with consumers as they encourage a sense of personal responsibility and control. Being agents of self-change, and mastering a problem through personal initiative and effort, greatly enhances feelings of self-worth and competence.

Most mothers spend a considerable amount of time sharing information and comparing their experiences with those of other mothers. Prevalent images of motherhood rarely reflect the actual 'mothering' experience of women, and the stark contrast between the fantasy and the reality demands an adjustment process postnatally. When people's experiences are at odds with the norm for their particular social group, their sense of identity and self-esteem is threatened. One of the key benefits of group membership in such a situation is 'normalisation' and there is no professional equivalent to affiliation with others in a similar situation. In fact when stigmatisation and loss of self-esteem are major components or consequences of any problem, a self-help group is considered the treatment of choice.

Another key factor in promoting adjustment or recovery is support – the comfort, reassurance and advice that are essential to all human care giving. Research has shown that the specific 'helping' activities which occur within the safety of a cohesive group are comparable to those occurring in a natural social setting, but of course they are more focused and open communication is actively encouraged. Group members are facilitated to share their experiences, thoughts and feelings more than is perhaps possible in their usual social group. Many mothers with postnatal depression report an increasing reluctance to talk with their family and friends. They perceive a growing impatience and a lack of understanding of their experience and they become discouraged by inappropriate responses. Having had similar experiences themselves, members of any self-help group are more able to empathise and communicate an understanding of the condition. Empathy is of great therapeutic value. The concern of the group also affirms the individual as a worthwhile person, reinforces their efforts to explore coping strategies and builds morale. There is also a wealth of knowledge within such a group, which empowers in situations where personal control and competence have been diminished.

There is a natural resistance to 'help seeking'. Whilst it is the norm when distress levels are very high (e.g. puerperal psychosis), and women are better at it than men, many women are very reluctant to seek help postnatally, even when their difficulties far exceed the ability of their family and social network to provide either practical or emotional support. Social contacts, and particularly partners and family, act as screening and referral agents as they transmit powerful attitudes about problems and problem solving. Keeping things in the family, not bothering the doctor, not believing in taking tablets, feeling that needing help is an admission of failure, are some common attitudes which prevent women seeking postnatal support.

Challenging societal attitudes through education and publicity is an important role for most self-help groups but equally important is ensuring that those who need help can actually meet each other. Most groups develop slowly through the trojan efforts of founder members. Having benefited from coming together to address their own difficulties, they then resolve to develop a larger organisation with a service orientation. Ironically as this happens, preserving the small group focus, which so benefited and motivated the pioneers, becomes more difficult, particularly when a self-limiting condition such as postnatal depression is involved. Nobody needs support for postnatal depression forever, and few who have recovered can maintain their commitment indefinitely. It becomes essential to have an active outreach programme, with strong encouragement from a central organisation for the formation of small local groups.

Professionals have an important contribution to make in developing and maintaining this programme. Being aware of local groups, actively endorsing their work, lending expertise, and encouraging clients to make contact are all important. Resistance to joining groups is significantly reduced when they are legitimised by acknowledged 'experts' in the field, or by other respected individuals or organisations. Good links do not only benefit self-help groups. Research shows that group members are not primarily those who lack personal resources or other sources of help, but are in fact people who use multiple sources of help. They tend to use professional help more effectively than the general population and consequently report a higher level of satisfaction with those services.

The ideal model is one in which everyone who has contact with mothers postnatally, from the doctor to the next-door neighbour, understands and appreciates the contribution each can make to minimise distress. Resources are then pooled, community networks develop which improve the level of accessible services for everyone, and most important from the psychological view point – women and their families are well informed and active participants in the process of recovery.

* * *

History of the Postnatal Distress Association of Ireland

The Postnatal Distress Support Group was set up in May 1989 by a woman called Bernie Brennan. She suffered puerperal psychosis after the births of her two daughters, and knew that she couldn't have been the only woman in Ireland who suffered this condition after birth. She placed an ad in *The Irish Times*, which was seen by a woman called Anne O'Connor (she herself had suffered PND a few years previously). Both women met in Bernie's sitting room that night in May. Both had something in common. They had suffered a depressive illness and recovered. A lot of it was due to their own self-determination in trying to get help for themselves.

That night the idea for support meetings and for a self-help voluntary group for women suffering PND was born. The aim was (and still is to this day) to offer support and friendship to women and their families suffering depression after childbirth. They placed a few notices around the city and organised a public meeting in the Well-Woman Centre, Leeson Street. It was well attended by PND sufferers, their families and recovered women. From the start the term depression was not used in naming the group, as it was felt it was a misleading term because frequently depression is not the symptom that leads the sufferer to get help.

The support meetings were held once a month at different venues throughout the city. Finally, after about a year, a permanent venue was secured for support meetings at the Dublin Central Mission in Abbey Street. The venue has remained the same to this day. The Support Group was and still is a totally voluntary organisation. Expenses were paid from generous donations – often the women themselves dipping into their own pockets. Gradually a core group of about five women emerged (all of whom had suffered and recovered from PND) and these women took responsibility for organising the Support Group meetings, and writing to maternity hospitals, GPs, etc. to let them know of their existence. They also took calls from women suffering from PND in their own homes, giving them reassurance and support. Every woman was given a listening ear.

In October 1991 the first conference of the PND support group was held in the Ormond Hotel, Dublin. It was a huge success and well-attended by the medical profession. Their first booklet, *Experiences of Postnatal Depression*, was launched at the conference by Monica Barnes TD. Out of it came the idea for posters (to advertise meetings) and the need to become an association and draw up a constitution. They changed the name to the Postnatal Distress Association of Ireland in May 1992. A committee of six women was formed to organise the 'business' of the association. The committee comprised a chairperson, secretary, treasurer and public relations officer. The first chairperson of the PNDAI was Anne O'Connor (one of the founder members), and she remained in that position until March 1994.

During this time support groups were set up around the country – Cork, Drogheda, Galway, Clare, Kilkenny and Wicklow, with two in Dublin – Abbey Street and Clondalkin. Unfortunately the Wicklow and Clare groups folded. But the others are still going strong and new groups have started in Wexford and Kilkenny. The *Mother to Mother* letter writing scheme is still being operated by Claire O'Dwyer in Co Clare.

As the association grew we needed to set ourselves up in an office. In November 1993 we were successful in obtaining a grant of £1,500 from the Department of Social Welfare to help us towards setting up an office. This was achieved in January 1994 when we acquired office space at the Carmichael Centre for Voluntary Groups in North Brunswick Street, Dublin 7.

We set up a phone-counselling helpline when some of the women on the committee did counselling courses. The medical profession began to see the value in our work and we began to give talks to GPs, women's groups, public health nurses, etc. In

October 1994 we held our second conference, 'Postnatal Depression as a family illness' at the Coombe Women's Hospital. Again, as in October 1994, it was a huge success, increasing the awareness of the condition of PND among the medical profession.

So, to the present time PND support meetings have been set up in the Coombe Women's Hospital (March 1995) and the Rotunda (October 1995).

* * *

How to Set Up a PND Self-Help Group

Step 1:

Advertise for any other women who have suffered PND and would be interested in helping to set up a self-help group. You can't do it alone. Ways of doing this include putting the advert in local newspapers, in windows of local shops, local health centres, baby clinics, maternity hospitals, GPs' waiting rooms, play groups. You could try using the local radio station to help get your message across.

Step 2:

The initial group should spend some time getting to know each other. Share experiences of where help has been sought and whether it has been received. This helps to build up trust within a group.

Step 3:

Find a venue for your meetings and set dates for those meetings, e.g. First Monday of the month. You may have to have your meetings in each others' homes until you gain access to a venue. They could be coffee mornings or evening meetings.

Step 4:

Set about advertising your meetings. Again place posters in all obvious local buildings. Let the professionals know of your existence, i.e. local GP, maternity hospital, health clinic, social workers, psychiatrists, etc.

Step 5:

You could offer a helpline service as long as each member is willing to take turn in answering the phone. No one member should be left to do everything. Remember you do have your own family to consider as well. Again the phone numbers could be put on your posters (PNDAI will supply such posters and leaflets). (see p. 88)

Step 6:

Naturally all calls and meetings follow a strong code of confidentiality. This helps the woman to trust the members of the group and she will then open up and talk more freely about her feelings.

Step 7:

You could organise 'information nights' in a local hall where members of the group along with a panel of professionals could give talks on PND and other topics relevant to the illness. You could also do counselling courses on how to answer phones, how best to listen, etc.

Remember to encourage the participation of the partners as they too need help in dealing with this time of stress in their lives.

So, in conclusion, the main elements needed for a good self-help group are:

- Advertisement
- Dedication
- Confidentiality
- Listening Skills
- A venue
- An ability to step back from the situation – not to become too involved
- Patience when the going gets tough.

You could seek grants to help pay for the group's outlays. Again PNDAI would be glad to offer advice on this subject.

Towards a PND policy

What improvements could be made in the treatment of PND sufferers?

The most difficult problems we face are secrecy, ignorance and guilt. If 10-15% of Irish women suffer with some form of postnatal depression then why do we hear so little about it? The first line of secrecy is within the home. Many women bottle up their misery deep within themselves and keep up a good exterior act at great cost to themselves. Others try to voice their feelings but may be silenced by the reactions of partners, friends and neighbours. Mental and physical isolation can hit a mother whether she is in a sprawling housing estate, a Dublin townhouse or on an isolated farm. The stigma of any mental illness cuts into all strands of Irish society.

PND does not just affect society's stereotype of the incompetent first time mother. In fact second, third of fourth time mothers can go through an episode of postnatal distress which may be even harder to recognise and treat. All Irish mothers deserve a far greater degree of practical and emotional support.

In an ideal world there would be much more information, education and understanding on all issues of mental health. Information on PND should be accessible and commonplace. We need to discuss the possible difficulties of pregnancy and the postnatal period more realistically in antenatal classes and at other times with family, friends and neighbours. Knowledge will always stand to us, whether we try to put it into practice for ourselves or in our dealings with others. Friends and family must also be knowledgeable about PND if we are to take any steps away from the current attitudes like 'buck up, what have you got to be depressed about?'

There must be a priority on highlighting the prevalence of PND through an education and publicity programme. Antenatal classes are the obvious place to start.

Mothers with puerperal psychosis or severe PND who need hospital care should be treated, if at all possible, in mother and baby units. The women who do end up needing hospitalisation often feel totally isolated in mainstream psychiatric hospitals and are further distressed by being separated from their babies. Therefore in allocation of funds for women's healthcare adequate funding should be made available for mother and baby units. These units don't necessarily have to be attached to maternity hospitals. They could be located in areas of maximum population growth. They would provide a bed for the mother and her baby, having been referred by both a GP and psychiatrist. There would be both medical and nursing expertise on hand to deal efficiently and knowledgeably with the patient. This could also provide a location for the training of medical students and student psychiatric nurses.

Maternity hospitals need to be in tune with the individual needs of each woman in childbirth. Many PND sufferers trace back their difficulties to an unsatisfactory birth experience. Doctors, midwives, psychiatrists, social workers and public health nurses all need an improved training and knowledge of the various forms of post-natal illness.

Women should have the option of staying longer than the 3-5 days usually allowed to them. This is especially important because PND is much less dramatic than puerperal psychosis and therefore can be easily missed in the days immediately following birth.

The excellent Community Mothers Scheme should be extended nationwide with appropriate funding to all health boards.

Visits from the public health nurse must not only be 'baby centred' but should also enquire into the physical and mental health of the mother. Postnatal backup should be expanded for all mothers, not only those with definite problems. Women should be encouraged to go back to their maternity hospital, not only for the six weeks check up, but for a wider service covering a range of postnatal areas.

Women should be encouraged and facilitated in their efforts to meet up with other women. Specialised support groups deserve practical help in the provision of meeting rooms in health clinics or hospitals offering maternity services. Mothers with post natal illness and those struggling to recover would benefit from participation in many types of voluntary groups. These groups deserve government funding and support.

There must be an improved awareness of the importance of counselling for PND sufferers and their families. GPs must either find time themselves or refer a patient on to someone with more specialised skills.

Many women wrongly believe that anti-depressants are addictive and they group them together with tranquillisers such as valium. Doctors must take the time to explain the various forms of medication that could be used whilst realising that medication is just one part of a strategy towards recovery.

The pressures to go back to work or to stay away from work are equally damaging to a mother's mental health after having a baby. We must work towards more economic and social support for mothers as they face the conflicting dilemmas which motherhood can bring. We should take a good look at our maternity leave structure and consider paternity leave. PND is not simply a woman's complaint. We must recognise the pain and distress that it causes to partners, families and friends. We all need greater education and a more realistic attitude to childbirth and parenting. All mothers deserve support. Those families who have experienced some form of postnatal distress must try to open up to those around them to help speed their own recovery and also to share the insights they discover through coping with this illness. The secrecy surrounding PND must be dispelled.

The people involved in advertising products aimed at pregnant or new mothers should take a hard look at the images they are presenting. New mothers feel they have to live up to this 'superwoman – everything is under control' image when we all know the reality is very different.

There should be more media coverage of PND, but not only of the negative aspects of the illness. A more positive and hopeful message should be communicated to the public at large concerning PND and women's mental health in general.

It is about time that all types of depression, not only PND, were de-stigmatised in Ireland. Depression is an illness like any other illness. The sufferers should be offered the respect and dignity they deserve. A positive health policy to educate the younger generations into realising that you should not have to be ashamed of your depression would be an excellent way forward.

In conclusion

Government, maternity services and voluntary organisations must all work together to provide greater levels of support for individuals and families suffering PND.

PND shouldn't be a wasted negative experience for the woman or her family.

APPENDIX I

Postnatal Depression

Vivette Glover DSc
Department of Paediatrics, Queen Charlotte's and Chelsea Hospital, Goldhawk Road, London W60XG

Introduction

Postnatal depression is an undertreated condition, which can cause considerable distress to the subject herself and those around her. It can also have a disturbing influence on family life. However postnatal depression is also a subject about which there are several common beliefs, for which there is no evidence. First, that it is much more common than antenatal depression. In fact antenatal depression is also very common, and much less discussed. Secondly, that it is mainly caused by hormones. This may well be true, but there is, as yet, very little evidence for it. Others believe that it is predominantly caused by psycho-social factors. Again this may be true, and there is much evidence that emotional support or lack of it can play a part, but it is not known to what extent this is the whole story. That it is best treated with progesterone, and that it develops insidiously by about the sixth postpartum week, are also frequently believed, again with no well-documented evidence. Some researchers in the field have even begun to wonder whether postnatal depression exists at all.

Does postnatal depression exist?

It is often stated that about 10% of women suffer from postnatal depression, and indeed many studies have found that if women at six weeks or three months postpartum are screened for depression, about 10% are depressed. The problem is that in studies that have used similar methods for measuring depression, it has been shown that about 10% of well matched women who have not recently had a baby were also depressed. Many women in our community are depressed at any one time. These findings have led researchers to raise the question as to whether there is such an entity as postnatal depression at all.

However there does appear to be an increase in the development of *new* cases of depression in the immediate postpartum period. Cox et al have confirmed this in a recent study in which they have shown that the *incidence* (new cases) of new depression arising in the first five postpartum weeks is *three fold* greater than in well matched non postpartum women.

We have followed through a cohort of 189 women from the antenatal period to six weeks postpartum, at weekly intervals, and shown that in those depressed at six weeks postpartum, the depression arose in the first two postpartum weeks in about 50%. About half of the remainder had been depressed antenatally, and in the remaining quarter, the depression developed more slowly. This confirms that there *is* a subgroup with early onset postnatal depression, but that some women are depressed both antenatally and postnatally.

So how can we explain these apparently contradictory findings, that a particular group of women start to become depressed after having a baby, but the overall level of depression is the same as that in women who have not recently given birth? It is possible that in some women, the joy and involvement of having a baby protects against the depression that they might otherwise suffer from. Thus, having a baby may cause depression in some women and protect against it in others. Again, there is no evidence for this.

There is no controversy about the fact that women in the immediate postpartum period are at strong risk of very serious psychiatric disorder, and that admissions to psychiatric wards are substantially increased at this time. Postnatal psychosis affects about 0.2% of women and is usually of the depressive or manic depressive type. A personal or family history of manic depression is a strong risk factor.

There is also good evidence for the blues, a mild disorder with symptoms of crying, depression and lability of feelings which starts on the third to fifth postpartum day and lasts a few hours or a few days, and which affects 50-80% of women, depending on how it is measured.

What are the symptoms of postnatal depression?

Brice Pitt originally believed that postnatal depression was predominantly what is called 'atypical' depression. However it now appears to have the same range of symptoms as those that occur in depression at other times. It can range from mild to severe (with biological symptoms such as decrease in appetite and early morning wakening) to psychotic depression (losing touch with reality). In a recent study we found that about a quarter of women who were depressed six weeks postnatally, with a depression that had arisen postpartum, had the more severe biological type of symptom.

Detection

The Edinburgh Postnatal Depression Scale

The Edinburgh Postnatal Depression Scale (EPDS) has been developed specifically for use in the *puerperium*, approximately six weeks after the birth, while the other more generally used scales contain some items not suitable for these patients. The EPDS is a simple self-rating scale which has proved very popular and is increasingly used both to help primary health care workers with the identification of potential patients, and by research workers in this field.

Links between mood changes (the blues and the highs) in the first postpartum week and later depression

The blues. Both our group and others have shown that *severe* blues are a risk factor for later depression. Kendell et al showed that women who were depressed at three weeks postpartum had higher scores on depression and lability scales in the first postpartum week and that their symptoms continued to be significantly higher than those of a control group in the next two weeks, although there were considerable fluctuations in intensity. We have found that severe blues (affecting about 10% of women) are a strong risk factor for depression at six weeks postpartum.

The highs. Recent work has identified a further group at risk. These are the 10% of women who show symptoms of mild hypomania in the first week postpartum. The phenomenon has been called 'the highs'. Unlike the blues they start on day one, or immediately after labour. As well as feeling euphoric, such women have associated symptoms of feeling a need for less sleep than usual, feeling more active and talkative than usual, and have racing thoughts and trouble concentrating (see questionnaire on p. 83).

The highs can coexist with the blues but are usually separate from them. A significantly larger proportion of this group go on to suffer later depression than those with no psychopathology at this time.

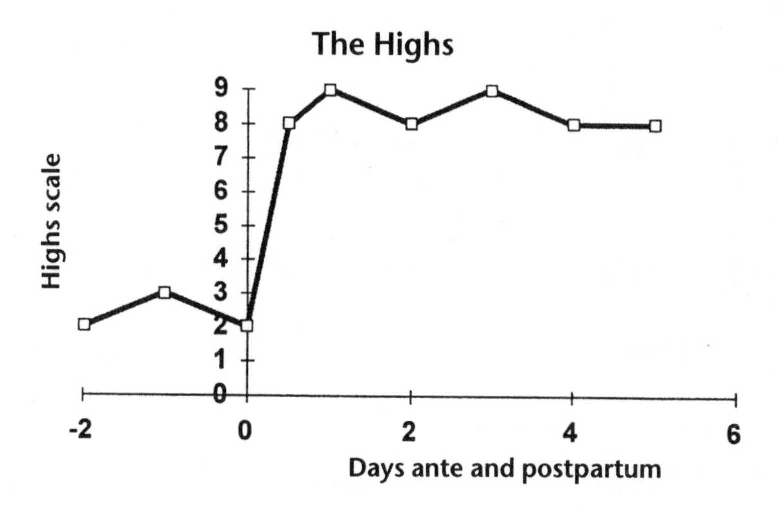

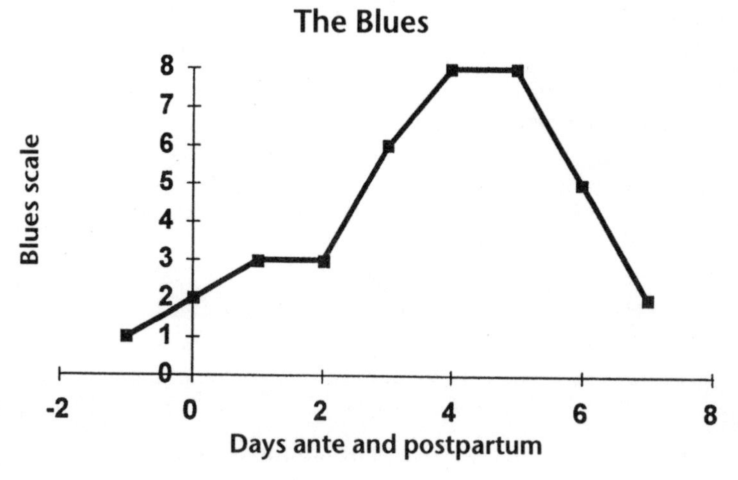

Causes

Hormonal causes

There are large changes in levels of progesterone, oestrogen, cortisol, and ß-endorphin at parturition, all of which are known to be psychoactive, to affect mood and psychological state.

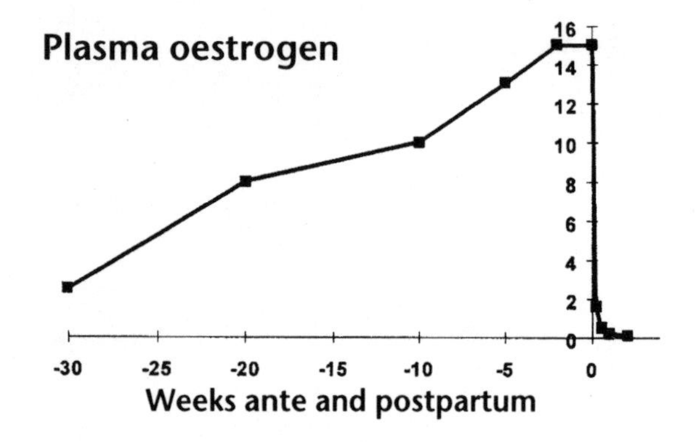

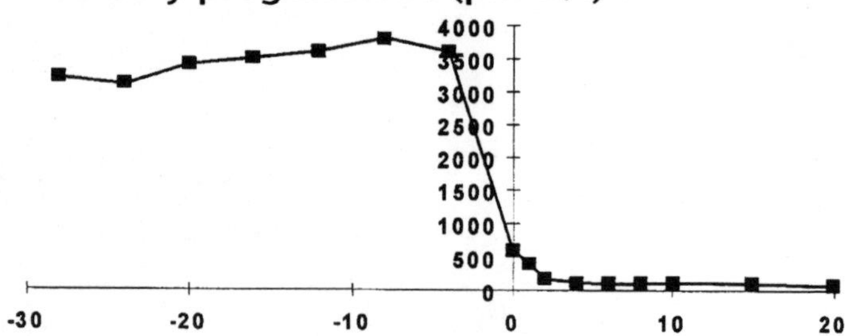

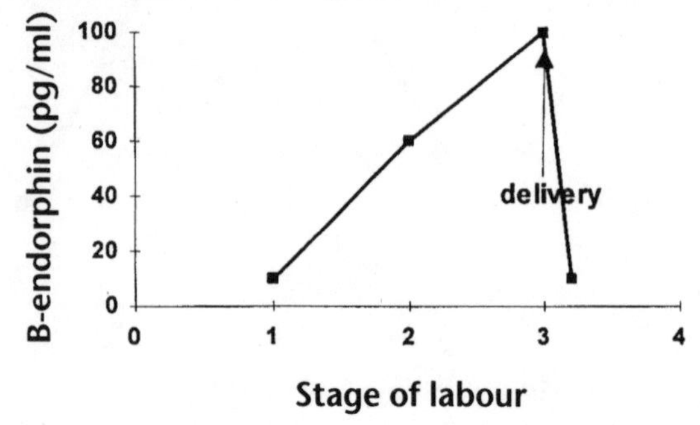

Progesterone and its metabolites are sedative and can reduce anxiety; oestrogen can be antidepressant; cortisol can cause depression and occasionally mania, as in Cushing's syndrome. ß-Endorphin can cause mania. It is almost surprising that more women do not experience profound changes of mood after having a baby. It is very plausible that a combination of these changes in hormone level contributes to the feelings of both euphoria and depression that many women feel in the postpartum period. However there is currently no evidence to link any of these hormonal changes directly with postnatal depression.

The degree of drop in progesterone level, from antenatal to postnatal, is weakly linked with the blues. Cortisol levels are raised in the blues, and reduced in the highs. Thus there is some evidence for a link between hormonal changes and the blues and highs which are in turn linked with postnatal depression.

In about 1% of women postnatal depression seems to be associated with thyroid dysfunction. This has a late onset, at between two and five months postpartum.

Personal or family history of depression

Several studies have found that a personal history of depression or emotional disorder is a risk factor. This could be due to either biological or psycho-social factors.

Psycho-social causes

Several studies have found that lack of support from partner, and life events contribute to postnatal depression. Low socio-economic status and a high neuroticsm score on the Eysenck Personality Questionnaire may also be risk factors. Thus psycho-social factors clearly play some part, but the extent of their contribution is unclear. A recent study showed that depression level during pregnancy, low socio-economic status, negative life events and a personal history of emotional disorder were all significant risk factors, but together only accounted for 26% of the variance in postpartum depressive symptomatology level (Bernazzani: presented at Marce Society 1994).

Time of onset

There is considerable variation in time of onset which is presumably linked to the heterogeneity of the disorder. Some women who are depressed postnatally have also been depressed continually during pregnancy, and in these cases the trigger cannot be the large hormonal changes of parturition. Psychiatric morbidity (as opposed to psychosis) may be only slightly less common during pregnancy than it is after it. In some individuals postnatal depression arises out of the blues. In 50% of cases of women depressed at six to twelve weeks postpartum, in a retrospective study they reported that depression arose in the first two postpartum weeks.

Depression can arise at any time in the first three or six postpartum months, as at any other time. Patients report that this often has an insidious onset. It is not clear that this all should be called postnatal depression, or at what time point a cut off should be drawn. Clinically, the treatment depends on symptoms and is independent of the time of onset.

Treatment

1. Non pharmacological treatment

A recent study has shown that counselling, cognitive behaviour therapy, and psychodynamic psychotherapy were all equally effective in advancing remission (Cooper and Murray; presented at the Marce Society 1994). Health visitors can be effectively trained to treat postnatal depression with basic counselling.

2. Pharmacological treatment

This is similar to the treatment of other depression of equivalent severity. Lofepramine is commonly used at the postnatal depression clinic at Queen Charlotte's and Chelsea Hospital.

3. Hormonal treatment

Progesterone is used frequently, and is often requested by patients who prefer a 'natural treatment'. It has only been used in open trials. There is no good evidence that it is better than placebo and there has been no placebo controlled trial.

In the pre-menstrual syndrome, for which it is also often used, there have been well conducted trials. All show that it is no better, or is actually worse, than placebo.

Oestradiol patches have been shown to be better than placebo in a controlled trial in postnatally depressed women. However optimal doses and side effects have not yet been established and oestrogen has not yet been used clinically.

Thyroid treatment may be appropriate in the small subgroup in whom depression is linked with thyroid dysfunction.

Mother baby bonding and effects on the child

Some depressed mothers have problems in bonding with their child, but this has been little researched so far. A new questionnaire is being developed which can be used to assess mother baby bonding (Kumar – in preparation). This is a subject that requires more research, as it is often very distressing for the mother not to feel the love for her baby that she expects to, and she may feel reluctant to talk about it. If she can be persuaded to discuss the problem, she can often be helped.

There is some statistical evidence that the children of mothers who have been depressed have various cognitive and behavioural difficulties, although most grow up quite normally. The effect seems to be particularly marked with boys. There is less agreement as to the importance of which particular time postpartum the mother was depressed, and the mechanism of the link is still unclear. Various different factors may be playing a part. These could be the direct effect of the mother's depression on her interaction with the child; genetic factors; or associated effects on the intrauterine development of the child.

A neglected condition

We have carried out a small study to investigate what help women who were depressed at six weeks postpartum had received. Twenty eight women completed the questionnaire. Of these, only six women (21%) had sought medical help. All respondents were invited to add their own comments. Typical examples were: *'I found nobody to talk to about how I felt.' 'Postnatal*

is not publicised enough generally.' 'Find an "instant
is horrible illness.'

References

Kendell, R.E., 'Emotional and physical factors in the genesis of puerperal mental disorders.' *Journal of Psychosomatic Research*, 1985. 29: p. 3-11.

Stein, G.S., 'The pattern of mental change and body weight change in the first postpartum week.' *Journal of Psychosomatic Research*, 1980. 24: p. 165-171.

Kennerley, H. and D. Gath, 'Maternity Blues: Detection and measurement by questionnaire.' *British Journal of Psychiatry*, 1989. 155: p. 356-362.

O'Hara, M.W., D.J. Neunaber, and E.M. Zekoski, 'A Prospective study of postpartum depression prevalence, course and predictive factors.' *Journal of Abnormal Psychology*, 1984.93(2): p. 158-171.

Ballard, C.G., et al., 'Prevalence of postnatal psychiatric morbidity in mothers and fathers.' *British Journal of Psychiatry*, 1994. 164: p. 782-788.

Kumar, R. and K.M. Robson, 'A prospective study of emotional disorders in childbearing women.' *British Journal of Psychiatry*, 1984. 144: p. 35-47.

Cox, J.L., D. Murray, and G. Chapman, 'A controlled study of the onset, duration and prevalence of postnatal depression.' *British Journal of Psychiatry*, 1993. 163: p. 27-31.

Pitt, B., '"Atypical" depression following childbirth.' *British Journal of Psychiatry*, 1968.14: p.1325-1337.

Hannah, P., et al., 'The tyramine test is not a marker for postnatal depression: early postpartum euphoria may be.' *Journal of Psychosomatic Obsterics and Gynaecology*, 1993. 14: p.295-304.

Cox, J.L., J.M. Holden, and R. Sagovsky, 'Detection of postnatal depression: development of the 10-item Edinburgh Depression Scale.' *British Journal of Psychiatry*, 1987.150: p.782-786.

Kendell, R.E., et al., 'Mood changes in the first three weeks after childbirth.' *Journal of Affective Disorders*, 1981. 3: p. 317-326.

Glover, V., et al., 'Mild hypomania (the highs) can be a feature of the first postpartum week: association with later depression.' *British Journal of Psychiatry*, 1994. 164: p.517-521.

Glover, V., 'Do biochemical factors play a part in postnatal depression?' *Progress in Neuro-Psychopharmacology and Biological Psychiatry*, 1992. 16: p. 605-615.

Harris, B., et al., 'Maternity blues and major endocrine changes: Cardiff puerperal mood and hormone study II.' *British Medical Journal*, 1994. 308: p. 949-953.

Okano, T. and J. Nomura, 'Endocrine study of the maternity blues.' *Progress in Neuro-Psychopharmacology and Biological Psychiatry*, 1992. 16: p. 921-932.

Harris, B., 'Postpartum thyroid disfunction and postnatal depression.' *Annals of Medicine*, 1993. 25: p. 215-216.

Marks, M.N., et al., 'Contribution of psychological and social factors to psychotic and non-psychotic relapse after childbirth in women with previous histories of affective disorder.' *Journal of Affective Disorders*, 1992. 29: p. 253-264.

Murray, L. and J. Cox, 'Screening for depression during pregnancy with the Edinburgh Depression Scale (EPDS).' *Journal of Infant Reproductive Psychology*, 1990. 8: p.99-107.

Holden, J.M., R. Sagovsky, and J.L. Cox, 'Counselling in a general practice setting: controlled study of health visitor intervention in treatment of postnatal depression.' *British Medical Journal*, 1989. 298: p. 223-226.

Henderson, A.F., et al., 'Treatment of severe postnatal depression with oestradiol skin patches.' *Lancet* ii, 1991.: p. 816-817.

Murray, L., 'The impact of postnatal depression on infant development.' *Journal of Child Psychology and Psychiatry*, 1992. 33: p. 543-561.

HIGHS QUESTIONNAIRE

In the *past 5 days*, have you felt any of the following conditions?

If you answer *yes* to any of these questions, please indicate on which days these feelings were present.

	Yes a lot	Yes a little	No	Days (1-5)
Have you felt elated (high or unusually cheerful)?				
Have you felt more active than usual?				
Have you felt more talkative than usual, or a pressure to keep on talking?				
Have your thoughts raced?				
Have you felt that you are a specially important person with special talents or abilities?				
Have you felt the need for less sleep?				
Have you had trouble concentrating because your attention keeps jumping to unimportant things around you?				

APPENDIX II

Organisations

Aware
Helping to Defeat Depression
Aware Administration Office, 147 Phibsborough Road, Dublin 7
Telephone: 01-8308449
Fax: 01-8306840
Helpline: 01-6791711 (open daily 10am-10pm)
Contact: Geraldine Browne

Cherish
2 Lower Pembroke Street, Dublin 2
Telephone: 01-6682744
Fax: 01-6682184

Cherish is an association of Single Parent Families working to improve the quality of life for single pregnant women and single parent families. Our aim is to encourage self-reliance through mutual support.

Gingerbread Ireland
29/30 Dame Street, Dublin 2
Telephone: 6710291
Fax: 6710352
Office Hours: 9.00-5.00
Meetings: New members every second and fourth Monday of the month at 8.30pm at YMCA, Aungier Street. Regular meeting every Tuesday night at 8.30pm at same venue.
Services we provide: mediation, legal advice, also people can drop into us for a chat which they will do when in distress.

GROW. Ireland's Community Mental Health Movement
National office: GROW Centre, 11 Liberty Street, Cork
Telephone: 021-277520

GROW believes that it has something to offer to everyone. Many people who join a group are looking for friendship and support, particularly if they have been struggling alone with their problems.

The group meeting allows people to share their difficulties and fears with others who have been in, and are coming from, similar situations. The group meeting in GROW consists of ordinary people sharing with each other their efforts to achieve and maintain good mental health.

Home Birth Centre of Ireland
25 Larkfield Grove, Terenure, Dublin 6W
Telephone: 01-4922565
A voluntary group which provides information and support to parents considering home as the place of birth for their babies. HBC also lobbies health boards and government departments to ensure home birth remains an option. Monthly meetings, a quarterly newsletter and an annual conference keep members and the public up to date with news on home birth.
Membership: £12.00 per annum, £7.00 unwaged families.

Irish Association for Counselling and Therapy
8 Cumberland Street, Dun Laoghaire, Co Dublin
Telephone: 01-2300061
Fax: 01-2300064
Contact: Grace O'Donnell, Administrator
IACT aims to promote counselling, to provide support for clients and counsellors, to set and maintain standards of counselling training and practice, and to increase the availability of counselling by trained and supervised counsellors. Services include referral, providing information, organising seminars, workshops and conferences.

Irish Association for Improvements in Maternity Services
Established: 1979
Contact: Berna O'Hanrahan, (Chairwoman) Raheen House, Meath Road, Bray, Co Wicklow
Telephone: 01-2864585
As a campaigning pressure group IAIMS has been in the forefront of the childbirth movement and has provided much of the

impetus for changes in childbirth practices in recent years. IAIMS receives many requests for advice and information from women throughout the country.
Consumer's Guide is available from address above at £1.00.

Irish Childbirth Trust – Cuidiú
President: Brenda O'Malley-Farrell, 52 Eaton Square, Terenure, Dublin 6W
The ICT is a mother-to-mother, non-professional community based support group which aims to help women to have their babies happily and free from fear, and to prepare families for the experience of childbirth and parenthood.

Irish Countrywomen's Association
(Bantracht na Tuaithe)
58 Merrion Road, Dublin 4
Telephone: 01-6680453
President: Bridin Twist
The association dates from 1910. Aimed at improving rural and urban life, the ICA has about 1,000 guilds throughout the country where local women meet to exchange ideas, for instruction in home and farm management, handcrafts, drama, music, verse-speaking and dancing. An Grianán, Termonfeckin, Co Louth is the residential adult education college of the ICA. In 1968 a Horticultural College for girls was officially opened at An Grianán.

ISANDS
Irish Stillbirth and Neonatal Death Society
Carmichael House, North Brunswick Street, Dublin 7
Contacts: Romy Moloney 01-2957785, Ann Canning 01-8373367
Providing support and information to those affected by stillbirth and neonatal death.

ISANDS help families who know their baby died prior to delivery or is likely to live only a short time after delivery; families recently bereaved through Stillbirth and Neonatal death; families whose babies died a number of years ago but due to social attitudes were not permitted to grieve; families considering another pregnancy.

ISIDA: Irish Sudden Infant Death Association
4 North Brunswick Street , Dublin 7
Freephone Nationwide Helpline 1-800-391391
General Office Enquiries: 01-8732711
Fax: 01-8726056

La Leche League of Ireland
Breastfeeding Help and Information
c/o 265 Martello, Portmarnock, Co Dublin
Fax: 01-8460699
Contact: Rhóda Uí Chonaire

Organises mother-to-mother support through groups around the country. Telephone counselling is available around the clock. See your local directory under La Leche League for phone numbers, or write directly to the address above.

Miscarriage Association of Ireland
Contact: Cathy Healy, 7 Tamarisk Way, Kilnamanagh, Dublin 24
Telephone: 01-4523992
We offer support and information following miscarriage by means of phone contact, monthly meetings and letters.
Meetings held in Molesworth Hall, Molesworth Place, Dublin 2 at 8pm on first Thursday of every month, excluding July and August. These are support group meetings only. No professional counselling is given.

Mothers to Mothers Pen Pal Support
Shrohill, Ennistymon, Co. Clare
Established: 1989
Contact: Claire O'Dwyer
This is a system where recovered PND sufferers write to women who are currently suffering from the illness.

National Women's Council of Ireland
32 Upper Fitzwilliam Street, Dublin 2
Telephone: 01-6615268
Chairwoman: Noreen Byrne
- highlights and promotes women's views and concerns on matters of public interest
- lobbies Government and policy-makers generally

- hosts workshops, seminars, conferences and events which promote public awareness of equality issues and influence change
- provides an information and advice service on women's rights
- liaises with organisations, groups and individuals to effect change.

Postnatal Distress Association of Ireland
Carmichael House, North Brunswick Street, Dublin 7
Phone: 01-8727172
Providing help and support for women and their families suffering with PND.

Premenstrual Syndrome and Post Natal Depression Support (East Belfast)
c/o 113 University Street, Belfast, BT7 1HP
Telephone: 01232-653209
Contact: Julia Crawford
Provides support and information to PMS and PND sufferers throughout the Province. Regular support group meetings held in Belfast.

Treoir (Federation of Services for Unmarried Parents and their Children)
36 Upper Rathmines Road, Dublin 6
Telephone: 01-4964155
Contact: Margaret Dromey
To improve the standards of care for unmarried parents and their children.

APPENDIX III

Hospital Guidelines

The author contacted all maternity units in Ireland requesting information on guidelines on treatment of PND sufferers. Those who did not respond were contacted a second time. Below are the replies received.

Bon Secours Hospital, Cork

Respondent: Sr Helena Mary Daly, Director of Nursing

If PND is detected while the mother is in hospital, the Consultant Obstetrician may request a Psychiatric consult, who in turn will combine postnatal care with the Obstetrician. If the Psychiatrist requests that a patient be transferred to a Psychiatric Hospital, same is carried out. Relatives are kept fully informed of every development. In addition to the immediate post natal care of the postnatal distress mother we also have a monthly postnatal distress Support Group held in the hospital, which we have found very helpful to the mothers.

Coombe Women's Hospital, Dolphin's Barn, Dublin 8

Telephone: 01-4537561

Respondent: Dr Siobhán Barry MD, MRCPsych, Visiting Consultant Psychiatrist

While a mother is in hospital, should there be concern about her being distressed, confused or not coping, an inpatient consultation with a Consultant Psychiatrist is organised. The Support Clinic for public patients is available to mothers who deliver in the hospital, and for up to 12 months after delivery. Those who have established, or long-standing difficulties might, following a first consultation at the clinic, be referred on to their local area psychiatric clinic. Referrals to the Clinic need to be made through a General Practitioner or the doctor at the CWH who has attended the mother. Regrettably, self referrals are not possible. The private psychiatric clinic runs on Friday afternoons. Patients are seen for assessment and treatment; second opinion consultations also take place. PNDAI run a coffee morning at the hospital (in the Academic Centre) on the first Wednesday of the month, and for some mothers this support and companionship is essential for their recovery.

Erinville Hospital, Western Road, Cork
Telephone: 021-275211
Respondent: Ms Mary O'Brien, Matron

If a woman presents while still in hospital we get a Psychiatric Consultant and subsequent follow-up. If she or her partner phone back to the hospital looking for help we advise the patient to go to her GP and it would be policy for us to notify the GP in question of the impending visit. We also display Post Natal Distress Association literature in appropriate places throughout the hospital. We would also notify the patient's Public Health Nurse of any problems in that area.

General Hospital, Monaghan
Telephone: 047-81811
Respondent: Sr Brendan, Matron

(a) If the mother presents with PND while in hospital this is dealt with by the nursing and medical staff of the ward. However, if the distress suffered by the mother is outside the ability of the staff to cope with, the Psychiatric Services are called to see the mother in the ward. (b) Should it be a case of postnatal depression, the Psychiatric Service are requested to see the patient in the ward. (c) On discharge from hospital the Community Care are notified and the mother is taken into the care of this service. (d) Should the person contact the hospital directly she is advised/requested to contact her GP.

Letterkenny General Hospital, Letterkenny, Co Donegal
Telephone 074-25888
Respondent: Seamus Gordon, Social Worker
Each case is dealt with on its own merit and, depending on the nature of the depression, could be referred, usually to a

GP, psychiatrist or social worker. We have just started a PND support group. Meetings are held on the first Tuesday of every month in the conference room of the General Hospital. Details about the group can be obtained through the hospital social workers.

Longford/Westmeath General Hospital, Mullingar,
Co Westmeath
Telephone: 044-40221
Respondent: Sr Anna Sloan, Matron

The midwife is the person who would deal with many distress signals and advise, listen and reassure the mother postnatally. Good antenatal care is of prime importance. When the midwife is unable to solve the distress the Obstetrician will then deal with this issue. When the distress is of a nature that needs further attention a Consultant Psychiatrist is called in for a consultation with the patient. When it is deemed necessary a transfer to a specialist hospital in consultation with the husband or nearest relative is arranged. When a person has left the hospital the mother often telephones the midwife for assistance and at this stage the midwife may advise the mother to contact her own family doctor and the Public Health Nurse.

Louth County Hospital, Dublin Road, Dundalk
Telephone: 042-34701/5
Respondent: Miss Mary Duff, Matron

Any patients with postnatal depression are generally referred to the Psychiatric Service by their General Practitioner. They are not referred back to the hospital as we have not got the appropriate service to offer.

Mount Carmel Hospital, Braemor Park, Churchtown, Dublin 14
Telephone: 01-4922211
Respondent: Ann J. Scott RGN, RM Ward Sister

1) The mother's obstetrician is contacted and if necessary he or she may suggest a visit from the hospital's psychotherapist prior to discharge. 2) The Public Health Nurse is contacted and made aware that the mother may be suffering from PND.

3) Her partner is made aware of the support and back-up she needs for the first few weeks after going home. 4) The ward sister usually keeps in contact with the mother for the first few weeks and lets her know she is always welcome back to the hospital. 5) Sadly, due to early discharge, many cases may be missed.

National Maternity Hospital, Holles Street, Dublin 2
Telephone: 01-6610277
Respondent: Dr Peter Boylan, Master

A specialist Psychological Assessment and Treatment Service for postnatal depression has been set up at the National Maternity Hospital. Mothers attending antenatal clinics are screened for the known risk factors associated with the development of postnatal depression and referred to the Consultant Psychiatrist for further assessment and appropriate treatment. Any mother who develops postnatal depression in the postpartum period will also receive appropriate assessment and treatment.

Ongoing treatment and follow up will be provided during the postpartum period either at the National Maternity Hospital or at the catchment area hospital, whichever is preferable. The majority of mothers with postnatal depression can be treated as outpatients.

There are definite plans to develop a Mother and Baby Unit to treat the small minority of mothers who require inpatient treatment. With the increasing recognition of the importance of postnatal depression, there are also definite plans to expand the services that are currently available and to develop improved links with General Practitioners, health visitors, and support groups for mothers who have suffered from postnatal depression.

Our Lady of Lourdes Hospital, Drogheda, Co Louth
Telephone: 041-37601
Respondent: M. J. Finnegan, Assistant Director in charge of Midwifery

Mothers presenting before discharge or who ring for advice after discharge are seen by a Consultant Psychiatrist from our local Psychiatric Hospital – St Brigid's Hospital, Ardee. The Psychiatrist is available to us at short notice and will visit the mother here. If there is a need for hospitalisation in a Psychiatric unit, mother and baby are transferred. Milder cases are treated here by the Psychiatrist and given an appointment on discharge. Mothers are also made aware of the local Postnatal Distress Group meetings.

Portiuncula Hospital, General & Maternity, Ballinasloe, Co Galway
Telephone: 0905-42140
Respondent: Mary Courtney, Matron

Each patient is assessed individually and a plan of care appropriate to that person's well being is developed.

Rotunda Hospital, Dublin 1
Telephone: 01-8730700
Respondent: M. A. Kelly, Matron

When a mother manifests postnatal depression while on postnatal ward the following procedures are carried out: (1) Midwife asks mother if she has any specific problem which may be causing depression. If so she endeavours to deal with problem. Medical Social Worker may be required. (2) If depressed for no reason, mother is seen by doctor, psychiatric appointment will be arranged and medication may be prescribed. Psychiatric follow-up will be arranged. Informed of Post Natal Depression Support Group. (3) Arrange early visit to patient's home by Public Health Nurse. Patient is informed that hospital may be contacted for help and advice at any time. (4) If parenting ability is in question or if mother feels unable to look after her infant, the baby will not be discharged into the house environment unless another adult is there to care for baby. (5) Mother is not discharged until *she feels* able to cope.

When a mother or partner telephone hospital following discharge seeking help with postnatal depression the following procedures are carried out: (1) Advise immediate visit to GP or back to the hospital for evaluation. (2) Inquire about the baby and patient's parenting ability. If unable to look after baby patient is advised to return to hospital with baby if in the first six weeks postpartum. (3) Psychiatric appointment will be arranged by GP or hospital psychiatrist. (4) Inform Mother of Postnatal Depression Support Group.

St Joseph's County Medical and Maternity Hospital,

Clonmel, Co Tipperary

Telephone: 052-21900/21091

Respondent: Mr R. Quinn, Matron

All mothers are told that they are welcome to contact the staff on the maternity ward at any time and particularly in the first six weeks after pregnancy. Following that contact they may be invited back to the hospital. Otherwise they are referred to their GP or the Public Health Nurse is asked to visit more regularly if it is required. While in hospital ongoing support is offered by midwives with a view to return visits following discharge. A psychiastrist may be asked to see a mother, particularly if severe depression sets in, although this would probably be done through the patient's GP.

St Munchins Regional Maternity Hospital, Ennis Road, Limerick
Telephone: 061-327455
Respondent: Mrs Ann McCarthy, Deputy Director of Nursing

In the event of postnatal distress being detected in a woman during her postnatal stay with us she is routinely seen by a member of the Obstetric Medical staff, who in turn will request a member of the Psychiatric Medical staff to review the patient. Prior to the woman being discharged from our care, her GP and Public Health Nurse are informed of her condition. We hope to set up a support group for the women of the Mid Western Health Board area suffering from PND.

Sligo General Hospital, The Mall, Sligo
Telephone: 071-71111
Respondent: Katherine J Craughwell, Director of Nursing

Patients who contact us after discharge are referred to the General Practitioner who makes whatever arrangements are necessary. They are also given the phone number of the

Postnatal Distress Association of Ireland. Patients who are distressed in hospital have their particular problem dealt with at the time, with whatever follow-up care required, arranged in the community.

Tralee General Hospital, Tralee, Co Kerry
Telephone: 066-26222
Respondent: Elizabeth Anne Heffernan, Sister, Post Natal Ward

In hospital: where staff are unable to resolve the distress, the patient is seen by the consultant. The assistance of the pastoral care team may be requested. If the distress continues, the assistance of the psychiatric team may be requested. Easy access is available, as this facility is already available on the premises. The woman may be seen within an hour of referral. (Some members of the pastoral care team are trained counsellors). Phone queries: asked to contact GP. If staff receiving the call are concerned, the Public Health Nurse is contacted and asked to visit.

University College Hospital, Galway
Telephone: 091-24222
Respondent: B A Howley, Matron

These mothers are seen by their Consultant as either in-patients or outpatients and where indicated referred for appropriate follow-up medical care.

Waterford Regional Hospital, Dunmore Road, Waterford
Telephone: 051-73321
Respondent: Ann Ellis

Patients identified on the postnatal ward, or who contact us on discharge from hospital with symptoms of postnatal depression are encouraged to return to hospital to speak with a midwife or obstetrician, or to contact their GP. If possible, we notify the patient's public health nurse and alert her to the situation. A note is made in the patient's chart to alert us to be more aware in future pregnancies. We find that many of our patients ring back to the ward for a 'chat' long after discharge if they feel the need. We are currently in the process of establishing a self-help group at the hospital.

Wexford General Hospital

Telephone: 053-42233

Respondent: Bernard J. Finnegan, Matron

The hospital is extremely interested in promoting help for our patients who suffer from postnatal distress. Monthly self-help meetings are held in the hospital.